LOGIC
PUZZLES

CLASSIC

LOGIC PUZZLES

By J. J. Mendoza Fernandez,

George J. Summers, Norman D. Willis

Main Street
A division of Sterling Publishing Co., Inc.
New York

Material in this collection was adapted from

Challenging False Logic Puzzles © 1997 by Norman D. Willis
Mind Bafflers © 1998 by George J. Summers
Quick-to-Solve Brainteasers © 1998 Sterling Publishing Co., Inc.
Little Giant Encyclopedia of Logic Puzzles © 2000 by Norman D. Willis

10 9 8 7 6 5 4 3 2 1

© 2003 by Sterling Publishing Co., Inc.
Published by Sterling Publishing Co., Inc.
387 Park Avenue South, New York, NY 10016
Distributed in Canada by Sterling Publishing
c/o Canadian Manda Group, One Atlantic Avenue, Suite 105
Toronto, Ontario, Canada M6K 3E7
Distributed in Great Britain by Chrysalis Books
64 Brewery Road, London N7 9NT, England
Distributed in Australia by Capricorn Link (Australia) Pty. Ltd.
P.O. Box 704, Windsor, NSW 2756, Australia

Printed in China
All rights reserved

Sterling ISBN 1-4027-1063-1

CLASSIC LOGIC PUZZLES

CONTENTS

INTRODUCTION

Solving logic puzzles is an active way of developing your thinking power. The puzzles in this book are all of a formal logic nature, requiring that you think a problem through and reason deductively in arriving at the solution.

Each section in this book contains a different type of logic puzzle, and each presents a different kind of challenge. Use trial and error as a method in solving these logic puzzles. The information provided will afford a number of alternatives. Assume each in turn leads to the correct solution, and look for contradictions. When you have discarded unsatisfactory assumptions, what remains is the solution.

Diagrams are of value to aid in organizing and analyzing your assumptions. Suggested diagrams to use are provided either within the puzzles themselves or in "Hints" or "Solution Scheme" pages at the end of the section.

Whether or not you are new to logic puzzle solving, you will find many in this book that challenge your reasoning ability. As you gain experience solving them, you will find yourself meeting the challenge of more difficult puzzles, and you will enjoy the satisfaction that comes from successfully arriving at the correct solutions.

The puzzles range widely in degree of difficulty. Each section begins with the least difficult of a given type of puzzle and then they progress in difficulty.

PART I
WARMING UP

WARMING UP

These puzzles offer statements that provide limited amounts of pertinent information. Just enough information is available in each puzzle to enable you to find the solution. The puzzles are divided into three types, as follows:

A's: The statements within the puzzles in this part are all true and contribute information to help you solve each puzzle.

B's: Each puzzle in this part includes a false statement. To arrive at the correct solution, you will need to determine which statement is false, and discard it.

C's: The statements within each puzzle in this part are all false except one. It will be necessary to identify the true statement in order to solve the puzzle.

THE A'S

The statements given in these puzzles
are all true—no lies, no tricks. The information
will guide you logically to the solutions.

1A - FOUR VEHICLES

The Terrill family includes Mr. and Mrs. Terrill and their teenage son, Johnny. The family owns four vehicles: a roadster, a sedan, a popular new sports-utility vehicle, and a pickup truck. What vehicle is the usual transportation for each family member, and what is the color of each of the four vehicles?

1. Mr. Terrill drives the white vehicle, which is not the sedan, to and from work daily.
2. The truck has fewer miles on it than the yellow vehicle, the green vehicle, or the white vehicle.
3. The vehicle Johnny drives to school is not the roadster.
4. One vehicle, which is green, is over 50 years old and is used only during antique car rallies.
5. Mrs. Terrill prefers to drive the red vehicle.

	color	vehicle
Mr. Terrill		
Mrs. Terrill		
Johnny		
extra car		

Solution on page 177.

2A - HALLOWEEN COSTUMES

For Halloween one year four children, who are good friends, decided that they would each wear a different costume for trick-or-treating together. One wore a skeleton costume, one dressed up as a pirate, one wore a scary witch costume, and one dressed up as Robin Hood.

From the statements that follow, what is the surname (one is Finley) of each child, and what was the costume each wore?

1. Jimmy and Molly, neither of whom wore a pirate costume or a witch costume, are brother and sister.

2. The Smith boy lives across the street from Jimmy and Molly, he didn't wear a witch costume.

3. Billy lives several blocks away, and he didn't wear a pirate costume.

4. The one who wore a skeleton costume was the hit of the evening. He was not Sam.

5. One of the Dixons wore a Robin Hood costume.

	surname	costume
Billy		
Jimmy		
Molly		
Sam		

Solution on page 178.

3A - GOLFING COUPLES

Two married couples played a round of golf together. No two golfers had the same score, although the combined score of Mr. and Mrs. Albert was 187, the same as that of Mr. and Mrs. Baker.

From the statements below, determine the first name (one is Harry), surname, and score of each of the four players.

1. George didn't have the lowest score of the four players, but it was lower than the average score.
2. Kathryn's score was three strokes higher than Carol's.
3. There was only one stroke difference between the scores of Mr. and Mrs. Albert.
4. The average score of the two men was two strokes higher than the average score of the two women.

	surname	score
Carol		
George		
Harry		
Kathryn		

Solution on pages 178–179.

4A - VACATION TRIPS

Three couples from Santa Fe, New Mexico, planned vacation trips, each couple to a different location. The three destinations were Atlanta, GA, Tucson, AZ, and Santa Barbara, CA.

From the following statements, determine the first names (one is James and one is Jean) of the indivi-duals and the surnames (one is Anderson) of each couple, and their destination.

1. Joyce said that they were going east to visit relatives.
2. Jack and his wife planned a golfing trip to Tucson.
3. John, his wife, and the Abernathys discussed their trips west while playing bridge together.
4. The Adamses don't play bridge.
5. Joan is not an Abernathy.

	surname	destination
Jack		
James		
Jean		
Joan		
John		
Joyce		

Solution on page 179.

5A - ACCOMPLISHED SISTERS

Four sisters, daughters of a Canadian diplomat, are musicians and also fluent in four European languages. Each plays a different musical instrument (the four instruments are the clarinet, the flute, the piano, and the violin) and each speaks a different language.

From the statements below, which sister plays which instrument and speaks which language (one is Italian)?

1. The sister who plays the clarinet does not speak French or German.

2. The sister who speaks Spanish especially likes her musical instrument, as she doesn't have to carry it to her music lessons.

3. Sheri doesn't speak German or Spanish, nor does she play the clarinet.

4. Ellen is not the girl who speaks German.

5. Neither Theresa, who doesn't play the flute, nor Ellen plays the clarinet.

	instrument	language
Ellen		
Renee		
Sheri		
Theresa		

Solution on page 180.

6A - SUMMER FUN

One summer day, four children were engaged in some outdoor fun. Two were five years old. Of the other two, one was six and the other was seven.

From the statements that follow, determine the age of each child and the outdoor activity in which each was engaged. One was flying a kite, one was playing with a dog, and two were playing catch.

1. Neither Ted nor the one who was flying a kite is the oldest.

2. Neither of the two youngest was flying a kite.

3. Theresa is older than the boy with whom she was playing catch.

4. Neither Tony nor the child who is six was playing with a dog.

5. Timmy, who is not the oldest, was not playing catch; nor was Ted, who is not older than Timmy.

	age	activity
Ted		
Theresa		
Timmy		
Tony		

Solution on page 181.

THE B'S

In this next section, the puzzles each contain
a series of statements. However, in each of these puzzles
you will find that one statement is false. It will be necessary for
you to identify the false one in order to
solve the puzzle.

1B - THE MIDVILLE MUDDLERS

The Midville Muddlers baseball team depends on four players to score most of their runs. The positions of the four are the three outfielders (right fielder, center fielder, and left fielder) and the catcher. From the statements that follow, determine the first name (Henry, Ken, Leo, or Stan), surname (one is Dodson), position, and batting average of each player. (Their batting averages are .280, .295, .310, and .325.)

first name	surname	position	batting avg.

One of the following statements is false.

1. Neither Leo nor the catcher has a batting average over .300.
2. Three who are neighbors are Clements, the rightfielder, and the player who bats .325.
3. The center fielder bats .295.
4. Stan's batting average is 30 points higher than that ofKen, who does not live near any of the other three.
5. Brooks and Henry, who is not Ashley, both bat over .300 and are in competition to see which will scorethe most runs this season.
6. Henry, who is neither the right fielder nor the leftfielder, has a lower batting average than the catcher.

Solution on page 182.

2B - FISHING VACATION PLANS

Carl and three of his friends who are avid fishermen decided to visit four of the world's finest sport fishing locations over a period of four years. Each friend had a different favorite location, so they chose the order in which they would take the trips by drawing the place names from a hat. Based on the statements below, what is the first name (Andy, Bill, Carl, or Dennis) and surname (one is Cole) of each friend, what was the favorite fishing location of each, and what was the order in which the trips were to be taken?

first name	surname	favorite location	order of trips

One of the statements below is false.

1. Andy and Barrott work for the same company; Bill is self-employed.

2. The Iceland trip was planned for the year before the Alaska trip, which was not Andy's favorite destination.

3. Carl and Barrott and their wives frequently play bridge together.

4. Whelan's favorite fishing location was the third trip, which was neither Patagonia nor New Zealand.

5. Whelan and Cole are married; the other two are not.

6. Dennis was disappointed that his favorite destination, New Zealand, was not to be the first; Crowley's favorite destination was planned for the last trip, so he was unsympathetic.

7. Barrott's favorite destination was the first.

Solution on page 183.

3B - WHITE-WATER RAFTING

Eight friends decided to try white-water rafting on a nearby river. They rented four two-person rafts; one was yellow, one was green, one was red, and one was blue. They selected partners for the four rafts and agreed on a destination at the end of a white-water run. Based on the following statements, one of which is false, what is the first name (Alan, Don, Frank, Henry, LeRoy, Paul, Phil, or Walt) and surname (Cook, Gladstone, Hawley, Hughes, O'Brien, Sands, Smith, or Wilson) of each of the friends; which were partners on the four rafts; and what color raft was used by each?

first name	surname	raft color

1. Phil and Cook, who were in the same raft, arrived at the destination without incident, but they were not the ones who finished first.

2. The red raft capsized and did not finish; the green raft was first to finish the white-water run.

3. O'Brien and LeRoy were not on the same raft.

4. Paul and Wilson finished last on their raft.

5. Fortunately, Henry is a good swimmer, and he helped his partner, Hughes (whose first name is not Walt), get to shore. They were able to recover their capsizedraft, but declined to finish the white-water run.

6. Frank was the first to select a raft, and he picked the yellow one. He and Hawley were on the second raft to finish the white-water run.

7. Alan and Hughes were on the same raft; they were the first to finish the white-water run.

8. LeRoy and Smith completed the run and were not in last place.

9. After their nearly tragic capsizing experience, Don and his partner, Gladstone, vowed not to set foot in another raft.

10. Alan did not care that he and his partner finished last; he was just glad that they made it.

Solution on page 184.

4B - SPELLING CONTEST

There were five finalists in the city schools spelling contest this year. They competed until four of the five misspelled a word, and the fifth one was declared the winner. From the following statements, one of which is false, what is the first name and surname (Jennings, Knudson, North, Olsen, or Salisbury) of each finalist; who missed what word; and what was the order in which they finished the competition?

first name	surname	word misspelled	place

1. North, who was not the one who misspelled "physiognomy," had not participated in a spelling contest before. He said he had not expected to do well.

2. "Vicissitude" was misspelled immediately after "bivouac" and immediately before "isthmus."

3. Eleanor was happy that her good friend Jennings was one of the two finalists in the contest.

4. Before Eric misspelled his word there were only two contestants left; he and Olsen had studied together in preparation for the contest.

5. Gordie, who lasted longer in the competition than Jennings, was not the winner.

6. Knudson, who is not Helen, was the first to misspell a word.

7. Helen, Jennings, and Olsen are neighbors.

8. Jennings told Lois that she could not sleep the night before the contest.

Solution on page 185.

5B - AUDUBON FIELD TRIP

Four married couples, who are members of the Audubon Society, undertook a bird-watching field trip to identify the varieties of birds to be observed in the local woods. To cover a sufficient area, each couple walked in a different direction. It was agreed that, for birds that were not common in the region, any sightings were to be recorded as to the time of the sighting and the name of the first person to see and identify the bird. At the end of the day, it was found that a different person was the first to sight each of eight uncommon birds.

From the following statements determine the first name and surname (Brinkley, Dwyer, Eng, or Valentine) of each member, and the variety of bird observed by each.

first name	surname	bird sighted

One of the following statements is false.

1. Neither James, Curtis, Mr. Brinkley, nor either of the Valentines was the first to sight a western tanager.

2. William was the first to sight a golden-crowned kinglet; he and his wife live near the Brinkleys.

3. Both Rosemary and Nancy, neither of whom is Valentine or Dwyer, were attending their first Audubon meeting and field trip, although both their spouses have been active members for several years.

4. Nancy was the second to sight a western tanager.

5. As program chairperson, Curtis's spouse is quite activeactive in the local Audubon Society chapter and arranges and attends all their outings.6.   A lazuli bunting was first sighted by Angela, who onlyattends an occasional Audubon Society chapter meeting or outing.

7. Nancy was disappointed that her husband, Curtis,sighted an acorn woodpecker before she sighted her bird.

8. A pine siskin, which was sighted early in the day, and a yellow warbler were first sighted by Mr. and Mrs. Dwyer, not necessarily in that order.

9. Harold was first to sight a white-crowned sparrow, at about the same time that Nancy sighted her bird in a different part of the woods; her bird was not a black-headed grosbeak.

10. Curtis was the last to sight his bird.

Solution on pages 186–187.

6B - CAR POOL

Six business people travel to and from work in a car pool van driven by a seventh person. The six are picked up each workday morning where they live and are returned home each evening.

From the statements that follow, for each of the business people determine the first name (one is Milton), surname (one is Altchech), occupation (one is a computer programmer), sequence of pickup in the morning, and sequence of drop-off in the evening. (Due to traffic patterns, the evening drop-off sequence is not necessarily the reverse of the morning pickup sequence.)

first name	surname	occupation	AM pickup	PM drop-off

One of the statements is false.

1. Amarol feels that she is fortunate to be the first one dropped off in the evening.

2. Neither Neal, Florence, Agassi, nor Atwater is the secretary.

3. Paul is the sixth to be picked up in the morning, but Avenal is the first to be dropped off in the evening.

4. The word processing supervisor is the third to be dropped off in the evening; the secretary is the sec- ond to be picked up in the morning and the fifth to be dropped off in the evening.

5. Adams, the attorney, dislikes having to be the first to be picked up in the morning and the last to be dropped off in the evening.

6. Gloria is picked up in the morning immediately after Neal and immediately before Paul. In the evening she is dropped off immediately after Avenal and immediately before Amarol, who is dropped off immediately before Evelyn.

7. Avenal, who is not the systems analyst, and Amarol are members of a men's choral group.

8. The personnel manager, who is not Atwater, is not the fourth or fifth to be picked up in the morning.

Solution on pages 187–189.

THE C'S

The following puzzles each contain a number of statements,
each of which provides a piece of information,
as did the puzzles in the previous two parts.
However, the statements within each puzzle in this part are false,
excepting only one statement which is true.
Your challenge in solving these puzzles is to first
identify the true statement.

Note: If any part of a statement is false, the entire statement is false.

1C - CLOUD FORMATIONS

One summer day, four children lay resting on a lawn. One noticed a cloud formation that looked like a flock of sheep. Another saw a rabbit; a third saw a lion; and the fourth spotted a cloud alligator.

From the following statements, of which only one is true, which child saw which animal (or animals) in the clouds?

1. Charlie did not see either an alligator or a rabbit.
2. Either Diane or Charlie saw a lion.
3. Becky did not see the flock of sheep until it was pointed out to her by one of the other children.
4. One of Andy and Diane spotted an alligator and the other spotted a flock of sheep.

cloud formation

Andy	
Becky	
Charlie	
Diane	

Solution on pages 190–191.

2C - FOUR VOCATIONS

	vocation			
	baker	butcher	carpenter	cook
Mr. Baker				
Mr. Butcher				
Mr. Carpenter				
Mr. Cook				

Four neighbors, Mr. Baker, Mr. Butcher, Mr. Cook, and Mr. Carpenter, are a baker, a butcher, a cook, and a carpenter, although none is employed in the vocation that is his namesake. Can you determine the vocation of each of the four?

Four of the statements below are false; only one is true.

1. Mr. Carpenter is the baker.
2. Neither Mr. Butcher nor Mr. Baker is the cook.
3. The butcher is neither Mr. Baker nor Mr. Carpenter.
4. Mr. Cook is the carpenter.
5. Mr. Butcher is the baker.

Solution on pages 191–192.

3C - FRIENDS AND CATS

Three good friends, who love cats, have each named their cat after one of the other friends. Of the clues that follow, only one is true; the others are false.

Which friend owns which cat?

1. Candy's cat is named either Dody or Alice.

2. Betsy's cat is named Alice.

3. Either the cat named Candy or the cat named Betsy is owned by Dody.

4. Neither the cat named Betsy nor the cat named Candy belongs to Alice.

5. The cat named Dody does not belong to Candy or Betsy.

Solution on pages 192–193.

4C - THE MOUNTAINTOP HERMITS

Four brothers decided years ago that a hermit's life was for them. The world had gotten too fast and complicated, what with internal combustion engines, wireless communications, and people telling you what to do.

They settled in a mountain range in the South-west, and each built a shelter on a separate mountaintop. One shelter faced north, one south, one east, and one west. They agreed to get together to share experiences on a regular basis. They met at one brother's shelter every spring, a second brother's shelter every summer, the third shelter every fall, and the fourth shelter every winter.

From the several statements below, which brother settled on which mountaintop, and what season of the year did they meet at each brother's shelter?

	shelter direction	host season
Billy		
Homer		
Jacob		
Willy		

Only one of the following statements is true.

1. Billy's shelter did not face south, nor was his shelter the location for the winter meetings.

2. Their summer meetings were not at the shelter that faced north or the shelter that faced south.

3. Homer hosted the fall, winter, or summer meetings, and either he or Billy lived in the shelter that faced east and the other lived in the shelter that faced west.

4. Either Jacob or Willy, whose shelter faced west, hosted the summer meetings.

5. The fall meetings were hosted by Jacob, whose shelter faced south.

Solution on pages 194–195.

5C - SAILBOAT RACE

Five couples enjoy sailboating, and they get together frequently to race each other. On one such occasion, two of their boats finished the race in a dead heat for first place, with the other three boats close behind.

From the following clues, which two finished in a tie for first place and which boats finished third, fourth, and fifth?

finish place

Smiths	
Stahls	
Stanfords	
Steinbergs	
Stewarts	

One statement is true; the others are false.

1. The Steinbergs were neither one of the two who finished in a dead heat for first place, nor the couple who finished in third place.

2. The Stanfords finished immediately behind the two who tied for first place.

3. The Stewarts did not finish either ahead of the Stanfords or behind the Smiths.

4. The Smiths finished two places ahead of the Stanfords, and immediately behind the two first- place finishers.

5. The Standfords did not finish in either fourth place or fifth place.

6. The Stahls finished ahead of both the Smiths and the Steinbergs.

Solution on pages 195–197.

6C - JAZZ COMBO

A jazz group plays three nights a week at Johnny's Seven Seas Restaurant. There are five members of the band: a tenor saxophone player, a piano player, a guitar player, a string bass player, and a drummer. From the statements that follow, only one of which is true, who plays which instrument?

1. The saxophone player frequently receives requests to play "Crazy Rhythm," which is one of her favorites.

2. Steve plays neither the piano nor the bass.

3. The guitar man is neither Al nor Ansel, who doesn't play the piano.

4. Ansel does not play the guitar, the piano, or the bass.

5. The drums are not played by Caroline, Ansel, or Roger.

6. The saxophone is not played by Roger or Al.

7. The drums are played by Steve, Ansel, or Al.

instrument

Ansel	
Caroline	
Al	
Roger	
Steve	

Solution on pages 197–198.

PART II
FALSE LOGIC

FALSE LOGIC

Logic puzzles involve the application of deductive reasoning. They are fun because they are challenging, and the challenge lies in forming conclusions based on the selective information afforded by each puzzle and arriving at a solution. The puzzles in this section all contain false statements that must be identified before you can achieve the correct solutions. Solving and enjoying these puzzles will help strengthen your mental powers and your ability to think logically—they have been developed with this in mind.

In solving puzzles, it is important to follow a sound method of analysis, including trial and error. After all the alternatives in a puzzle are clear to you, assume that each one in turn is correct, and test each against the puzzles considerations. Eliminate those assumptions that reveal inconsistencies or contradictions, and what remains is the solution. It will be helpful to use a diagram to aid in your analysis and in organizing tentative conclusions. There is a sample diagram given at the beginning of the section that can be adapted to be helpful in solving other puzzles of the same type.

THE CASES OF
INSPECTOR DETWEILER

There are some within Inspector Detweiler's shire who do not always obey the laws. This extraordinary sleuth has been faced with several crimes that require solving. Your challenge is to determine which suspects are telling the truth and which are not, and who are the guilty.

Construct diagrams listing the suspects on one axis and the statement numbers on the other. The example below will illustrate:

	1	2	3
A			
B			
C			

Indicate T or F as you form conclusions about each suspect's statements. Assume that each suspect, in turn, is guilty; test each assumption against the truthfulness of all statements.

WHO STOLE THE STRADIVARIUS?

A famous violinist was in town for a concert. While he was away from his room for a short time his favorite violin, a Stradivarius, was stolen. The inspector took immediate action, and through diligent research was able to identify four suspects. Each of them makes one statement as follows. The guilty one's statement is false; the other statements are true.

A. I was not in town at the the time of the theft.

B. C is the culprit.

C. B's statement is false.

D. C's statement is true.

Which one is guilty?

〰 **Consider** that the guilty suspect's statement is false; the other statements are true. Assume that each suspect in turn is guilty. In each case, is this consistent with the statements by the other suspects?

Solution on pages 199–200.

TWO PICKPOCKETS

Two pickpockets were plying their trade at the village fair. The inspector's review of the clues indicated that there were two culprits working together. He has interrogated four suspects who are known pickpockets. The two who are guilty each make only one true statement. Little is known as to the truthfulness of the statements made by the other two suspects. Determine the two who are guilty from their statements below:

A.   1.   B is one of the culprits.
　　　2.   C would never be guilty of such a crime.
　　　3.   D is a disreputable character and certainly could be one of the culprits.

B.   1.   A's first statement is true.
　　　2.   C is one of the culprits.
　　　3.   If C is not one of the culprits, then either A or D is guilty.

C.   1.   A's second statement is true.
　　　2.   B is not one of the guilty ones.
　　　3.   B's second statement is true.

D.   1.   A's third statement is true.
　　　2.   B's second statement is true.
　　　3.   C's second statement is false.

ᔕ **Consider** that the two who are guilty each make only one true statement. Assume that B is guilty; does this assumption hold up?

Solution on page 200.

THE POACHER

A closed hunting season in the forest has been declared. Hunting has been considered a source of food for some, and, consequently, poaching has become a problem. Inspector Detweiler has been requested to bring to a halt a series of illegal appropriations of game. Clues indicate that there is one culprit, and the inspector has identified four suspects. The four make statements below. The truthfulness of their statements is unknown, except that only one of the guilty suspect's statements is true.

> **A.** 1. D is innocent.
> 2. I am not the poacher.
> 3. Hunting is a source of food in these parts.
>
> **B.** 1. C's being a suspect is a case of mistaken identity.
> 2. A's second statement is true.
> 3. Not all of my statements are true.
>
> **C.** 1. I am not the poacher.
> 2. D is the poacher.
> 3. My being a suspect is not a case of mistaken identity.
>
> **D.** 1. A's statements are not all true.
> 2. At least one of C's statements is true.
> 3. I do not like to eat game.

Which one is the poacher?

✍ **Consider** that only one of the statements made by the guilty is true. Assume that B is guilty; test B's three statements against this assumption.

Solution on page 201.

PROPERTY DESTRUCTION AT THE VILLAGE INN

Five local villagers were having a late evening political discussion at the village gathering place. As the night wore on, the discussion deteriorated into a debate and then into an excessively noisy argument.

At this point, the proprietor attempted to intervene in order to quiet the disturbance. In the ensuing fracas, an expensive candelabrum was knocked over and broken. The five customers immediately vacated the premises.

Inspector Detweiler recorded the statements below in attempting to determine who broke the candelabrum. Not all of the statements are truthful. In fact, only one suspect makes no false statements.

Butcher

1. I was not even there.
2. The cobbler was looking for trouble; he did it.
3. The candlestick maker helped him do it.

Baker

1. I agree with the butcher's first statement.
2. The candlestick maker did not do it.

3. I agree with the butcher's second statement.

Candlestick Maker

1. I did not do it.
2. The butcher was there.
3. The baker did it.
4. The cobbler did not do it.

Blacksmith

1. If the proprietor had not intervened this would not have happened.
2. None of us is to blame.
3. The candlestick maker is innocent.
4. The cobbler did not do it.

Cobbler

1. I agree with the baker's third statement.
2. The candlestick maker did it.
3. I was not looking for trouble; I did not do it.
4. The baker did not do it.

Which one is guilty?

∽ **Consider** that only one suspect makes all true statements. Can you locate that suspect?

Solution on page 202.

TWO ARE GUILTY

In a series of thefts, it was found that there were two culprits working together. The inspector was able to identify five suspects, and the five each make two statements, below. One of the thieves makes two true statements. The other guilty one makes two false statements. Little is known as to the truthfulness of the statements made by the three innocent suspects.

A.   1.   I was nowhere near the scene of the crime that day.

         2.   B is innocent.

B.   1.   I am innocent.

         2.   E's first statement is false.

C.   1.   I have no idea who the guilty ones are.

         2.   D's statements are both false.

D.   1.   C's second statement is not true.

         2.   A is not guilty.

E.   1.   A and B are the thieves.

         2.   At least one of D's statements is true.

Which two are guilty?

〜 **Consider** that one of the two culprits makes two true statements; the other makes two false statements. Assume that A is guilty. Test this assumption against the statements made by the other four suspects.

Solution on page 203.

PICKPOCKET THEFTS

A notorious pickpocket had evaded apprehension for some time. The inspector redoubled his efforts to bring him to justice, and his keen detection work resulted in four suspects, all of whom were in town during the last known theft. One of them is guilty. Each makes three statements. If either A or C is guilty, each of the four suspects makes two true statements and one false statement. If either B or D is guilty, no two of the four suspects make the same number of true statements.

A.
1. I was out of town during the last known theft.
2. Neither D nor I did it.
3. C did not do it.

B.
1. A was in town during the last known theft.
2. I am innocent.
3. D is the guilty one.

C.
1. A is the pickpocket.
2. B's first statement is false.
3. B's third statement is false.

D.
1. The pickpocket deserves to be apprehended.
2. At least one of B's statements is false.
3. A is not guilty.

Who is guilty?

∽ **Consider** that if A or C is guilty, each suspect makes two true statements. If either B or D is guilty no two suspects make the same number of true statements. As you assume each in turn to be guilty, carefully assess the statements of the four suspects against these guidelines.

Solution on page 204.

D IS MISSING

A professional burglar has recently managed to actively pursue his criminal activities by targeting the homes of the most affluent villagers. The inspector is on the trail of the culprit and has identified four suspects, one of whom is missing. The other three are questioned; each makes two true statements and one false statement.

A. 1. I am not the burglar.
2. D has no alibi.
3. D went into hiding.

B. 1. A's first statement is true.
2. A's third statement is false.
3. D is not the burglar.

C. 1. I am not the burglar.
2. D has an alibi.
3. B's second statement is false.

Who is the burglar?

∽ **Consider** that each suspect makes two true and one false statement. Assume that C's second statement is his false one. Test this assumption against the statements by all three.

Solution on page 205.

THE UNLUCKY CAR THIEF

A car thief who had managed to evade the authorities in the past unknowingly took the automobile that belonged to Inspector Detweiler. The sleuth wasted no time and spared no effort in discovering and carefully examining the available clues. He was able to identify four suspects, with certainty that one of them was the culprit.

The four make the statements below. In total, six statements are true and six are false.

A.   1.   C and I had met many times before today.
      2.   B is guilty.
      3.   The car thief did not know it was the inspector's car.

B.   1.   D did not do it.
      2.   D's third statement is false.
      3.   I am innocent.

C.   1.   I had never met A before today.
      2.   B is not guilty.
      3.   D knows how to drive.

D.   1.   B's first statement is false.
      2.   I do not know how to drive.
      3.   A did it.

Which one is the car thief?

✍ **Consider** that there are six false statements. What can you tell from A's first statement and C's first statement, and from C's third statement and D's second statement?

Solution on page 206.

THE OLDEST OR THE YOUNGEST

A thief has been taking sheep from farmyards in the area, and there are four suspects. The inspector has been able to determine that the guilty one is either the oldest or the youngest of the four. They make the following statements, although each suspect makes only one true statement.

A.   1.   B is the oldest among us.
2.   The youngest among us is guilty.
3.   C is innocent

B.   1.   A is not the youngest.
2.   D is the guilty one.
3.   D is the youngest.

C.   1.   A is the youngest of the four of us.
2.   I am the oldest.
3.   D did not do it.

D.   1. The oldest among us is innocent.
2. B is guilty.
3. I am the youngest.

Which one is guilty?

A diagram, such as below, is suggested.

	1	2	3	oldest	youngest
A					
B					
C					
D					

෨ **Consider** that the guilty one is either the oldest or the youngest, and that each suspect makes only one true statement. Assume that A's first statement is true. Is this consistent with his second and third statements?

Solution on page 207.

THE DRAGONS OF LIDD

The greatest challenge and honor for a knight in the Kingdom of Lidd is to confront and slay a dragon. As a result, the dragon population in Lidd has been considerably reduced. Those dragons that have agreed to live peaceably have been put on the endangered species list and, by the king's decree, are protected.

Dragons in the Kingdom of Lidd are of two types. Some have reasoned accurately that devouring farm animals and their owners has attracted the attention of knights and is, in the long run, not a healthy thing for dragons to do. They have since totally refrained from this practice. These dragons are known as rationals, and they are the protected dragons.

Some dragons, on the other hand, have not learned to fear humans and continue in their traditional ways. These dragons are known as predators, and they are not protected from confrontations with knights.

In addition to being rationals or predators, dragons in Lidd are of two different colors, related to their veracity. Gray rational dragons always speak the truth; red rational dragons always lie. Red predator dragons always speak the truth; gray predator dragons always lie.

It is necessary for knights to know which dragons are rationals and which dragons are predators. To tell if a dragon is protected, it would help to know its color. However, there is an affliction endemic to all humans in Lidd: they are colorblind. To each knight, all dragons look gray. Therefore, it is important to ask a dragon his type and color, and to attempt to determine whether the answers are truthful or false.

Your challenge is to determine the color and type of each dragon encountered in the following puzzles.

TWO DRAGONS

A knight approaches two dragons and inquires as to the color and type of each. Gray rationals and red predators always tell the truth; red rationals and gray predators always lie. The dragons respond below:

A. 1. I am gray.
    2. B is a predator.

B. 1. A is a predator.
    2. I am a rational.

	A	B
color		
type		

Solution on page 208.

TWO MORE DRAGONS

Two knights in full armor approach two dragons and ask their types and colors. Gray rationals and red predators always speak the truth; red rationals and gray predators always lie. Their answers follow:

A.   1.   B and I are rationals.

        2.   Everything B says is false.

B.   1.   A and I are both predators.

        2.   I am red.

	A	B
color		
type		

Solution on pages 208–209.

THREE TO ONE

A lone knight cautiously approaches three dragons and inquires as to their types and colors. Gray rationals and red predators always speak the truth; red rationals and gray predators always lie. They respond as follows:

A.   1.   I am not a predator.
     2.   B is gray.

B.   1.   I am not a predator.
     2.   C is gray.
     3.   A's statements are true.

C.   1.   All three of us are protected by the king's decree.
     2.   A is red.
     3.   B is red.

	A	B	C
color			
type			

Solution on page 209.

THREE TO ONE AGAIN

A knight alone warily approaches three dragons and politely asks the type and color of each. Gray rationals and red predators always speak the truth; red rationals and gray predators always lie. Their answers are below:

A. 1. I am a rational, but I intend to eat youanyway.
    2. Neither B nor C is a rational.

B. 1. A is a rational that has spoken falsely.
    2. I am a rational.

C. 1. A and B are both predators.
    2. I am a gray rational.
    3. A's second statement is false.

	A	B	C
color			
type			

Solution on page 210.

WHOSE COLORS ARE THE SAME?

Two knights encounter three dragons and ask each his color and type. Gray rationals and red predators always speak the truth; red rationals and gray predators always lie. They respond below:

A. 1. I am a rational.
  2. Dragon C and I are not the same color.

B. 1. Dragon A is a rational.
  2. I am not red.

C. 1. Dragon B is a predator.
  2. Dragon A and I are the same color.

	A	B	C
color			
type			

Solution on pages 210–211.

THREE ON THREE

Three knights looking for adventure approach three dragons and ask for their colors and types. Gray rationals and red predators always speak the truth; red rationals and gray predators always lie. The three dragons answer below:

A. 1. B and C are predators.
2. I am a rational.

B. 1. Both A and C speak the truth.
2. I am not the same type as A.

C. 1. I am not the same type as A.
2. A and B are both gray.

	A	B	C
color			
type			

Solution on page 211.

ARE THERE ANY PREDATORS LEFT?

Two knights looking for some action approach three dragons. They inquire as to each dragon's type and color. Gray rationals and red predators always speak the truth; red rationals and gray predators always lie. The three dragons respond as follows:

A.   1.   Ask B what my type is; he will give you
            a truthful answer.
      2.   C is red.

B.   1.   A and I are both rationals.
      2.   C is a predator.

C.   1.   A and B are both predators.
      2.   B is gray.

	A	B	C
color			
type			

Solution on page 212.

HOW MANY ARE RATIONALS?

A lone knight happens on three large dragons and asks their colors and types. Gray rationals and red predators always speak the truth; red rationals and gray predators always lie. The three dragons respond below:

A. 1. Neither B nor I is gray.
    2. C claims to be red.
    3. Only two of the three of us speak the truth.

B. 1. I am a rational.
    2. A claims to be a predator.
    3. A's third statement is false.

C. 1. B is a predator.
    2. A claims to be a rational.

	A	B	C
color			
type			

Solution on pages 212–213.

THREE ON THREE AGAIN

Three knights seeking action confront three dragons and ask the type and color of each. Gray rationals and red predators always speak the truth; red rationals and grey predators always. The dragons' answers follow:

A.   1.   I am neither a red rational nor a gray predator.
     2.   C's statements are true.

B.   1.   A is either a red rational or a gray predator.
     2.   C would agree with me about A.

C.   1.   There is only one rational among the
              three of us, and it is I.
     2.   A is a red predator.

	A	B	C
color			
type			

Solution on page 213.

THE DRAGONS FROM WONK

Dragons from the adjacent Land of Wonk are either rationals or predators. However, they are all blue and they all lie. It is not unusual for knights to encounter blue dragons that have crossed into the Kingdom of Lidd.

ONE IS BLUE

Two knights looking for a confrontation encounter two dragons, one of which is blue, and ask their types and colors. Gray rationals and red predators always speak the truth; red rationals and gray predators always lie; blue rationals and blue predators always lie. The two dragons answer as follows:

A. 1. B is a predator.
  2. I am a rational.

B. 1. I am either a red rational or a gray predator.
  2. A is a predator.

	A	B
color		
type		

Solution on page 214.

TWO OF THREE ARE BLUE

Three dragons, two of which are blue, are approached by three knights, who inquire as to their types and colors. Gray rationals and red predators always speak the truth; red rationals and gray predators always lie; blue rationals and blue predators always lie. Their responses follow:

A.   1.   I am a rational.

B.   1.   I am not gray.
        2.   A and C are not the same type.

C.   1.   I am a predator

	A	B	C
color			
type			

Solution on page 214.

ONE OF THREE IS BLUE

This time, a lone knight confronts three dragons, one of which is blue. The knight asks their types and colors. As is known, gray rationals and red predators always speak the truth; red rationals and gray predators always lie; blue rationals and blue predators always lie. The three dragons reply as follows:

A. 1. B is blue.
2. I am the only rational among the three of us.

B. 1. C is blue.
2. C is a rational.

C. 1. A's first statement is false.
2. I am the blue dragon.

	A	B	C
color			
type			

Solution on page 215.

AT LEAST ONE IS A BLUE DRAGON

A group of four knights traveling together encounters four dragons, at least one of which is blue. The dragons are asked their types and colors. Gray rationals and red predators always speak the truth; red rationals and gray predators always lie; blue rationals and blue predators always lie.

A. 1. I am not a blue dragon.
2. If asked, C would state that D is a predator.
3. Only one of us is a blue dragon.

B. 1. C is a predator.
2. I am a blue dragon.

C. 1. I am a predator.
2. A is not a blue dragon.
3. Three of us are rationals.

D. 1. B is not a blue dragon.
2. If asked, B would state that A is a predator.

	A	B	C	D
color				
type				

Solution on pages 215–216.

HOW MANY BLUE DRAGONS?

A lone knight rounds a bend in the trail and finds himself facing four large dragons. He inquires as to their types and colors. Gray rationals and red predators always speak the truth; red rationals and gray predators always lie; blue rationals and blue predators always lie. Their answers follow:

A. 1. If you want to know my type, C will give you a true answer.
   2. D is blue.

B. 1. A and I are both rationals.
   2. Three of us are blue.

C. 1. If you want to know A's type, B will give you a true answer.
   2. Only one of us is blue.
   3. D's statements are false.

D. 1. Three of us are predators.
   2. A is a rational.
   3. A is not blue.

	A	B	C	D
color				
type				

Solution on page 217.

HYPERBOREA

Hyperborea was a wondrous land located north of Mount Olympus—home of the gods—and the inhabitants were much favored by the gods. It was a land of continual springtime, there was no disease, and life expectancy was a thousand years.

However, the people had unusual standards of veracity. Those living in the southern region, known as Sororeans, always spoke truthfully. Those who lived in the northern region, known as Nororeans, always spoke falsely. Hyperboreans living in the middle region, the Midroreans, were alternately truthful and false, or false and truthful. The following puzzles arise from their conflicting standards of veracity.

WHICH ROAD TO TAKE

The Hyperboreans were especially favored by the god Apollo, who visited them in disguise. Apollo wished to establish a meaningful dialogue with the inhabitants, but that was not easily accomplished.

Apollo, walking along, meets two inhabitants at a fork in the road, one road going to the left and the other to the right. The two Hyperboreans are known to be a Sororean, who always speaks truthfully, and a Nororean, who always speaks falsely. But which one is which? Apollo inquires as to which road he should take. The first inhabitant responds as follows:

A.   Take the road to the left.

Apollo, still a little uncertain, speaks to the first inhabitant again, and asks: "If I ask B which road to take, what will he say?"

A.   B will say to take the road to the left.

Which one of A and B is the Sororean, which one is the Nororean, and which road should Apollo take?

Indicate + (plus) or – (minus) in the diagram above as you draw conclusions regarding the veracity of the two Hyperboreans.

	Sororean	Nororean
A		
B		

Solution on page 218.

APOLLO GOES DOWN THE ROAD

A little confused, Apollo takes one of the two roads and meets two more inhabitants. This time he inquires as to the standard, or standards, of veracity of the two Hyperboreans. Sororeans always speak truthfully; Nororeans always speak falsely; and Midroreans make statements that are alternately truthful and false, or false and truthful. As to the group or groups to which these two speakers belong, little is known. They each make two responses:

A.   1.   I am a Nororean.
       2.   Neither of us is a Sororean.

B.   1.   I am a Sororean.
       2.   A is a Nororean.

What group or groups do A and B represent? Consider each statement and, as you draw conclusions, indicate + (plus) or − (minus) in the diagram.

	A	B
1		
2		
Sororean		
Nororean		
Midrorean		

Solution on pages 218–219.

SOME JUST LIKE TO BE DIFFICULT

Maybe Apollo needs to be more insistent. He does not seem to be making any headway at understanding the inhabitants. He decides to change his approach.

He meets three Hyperboreans and, with maybe a little less tact than he should use, he inquires as to their group or groups. Hyperboreans belong to different groups: Sororeans, who always speak truthfully; Nororeans, who always speak falsely; and Midroreans, who make statements that are alternately truthful and false, or false and truthful. As to these three, little is known as to their group or groups. They respond as follows:

A. 1. I am not a Sororean.
        2. C is a Midrorean.

B. 1. I am not a Nororean.
        2. A is a Sororean.

C. 1. I am not a Midrorean.
        2. B is a Nororean.

Which group or groups are represented by the three speakers?

	A	B	C
1			
2			
Sororean			
Nororean			
Midrorean			

Solution on page 219.

ONE SPEAKS TRUTHFULLY

Apollo, still trying to establish meaningful communication with the Hyperboreans, this time meets three more inhabitants. They are known as a Sororean, who always speaks truthfully; a Nororean, who always speaks falsely; and a Midrorean, who makes statements that are alternately truthful and false. Apollo now asks each of them which one is from which region. Their answers follow:

A. 1. C is the Nororean.
     2. B is not the Sororean.

B. 1. C is not the Sororean.
     2. A is the Nororean.

C. 1. B is the Midrorean.
     2. I am not the Nororean.

Which speaker represents which region?

	A	B	C
1			
2			
Sororean			
Nororean			
Midrorean			

Solution on pages 219–220.

APOLLO MAKES ONE LAST TRY

Apollo is ready to return to Mount Olympus, but he is willing to make one last try at establishing meaningful dialogue with the Hyperboreans. He approaches three inhabitants, who are known to be a Sororean, who always speaks truthfully; a Nororean, who always speaks falsely; and a Midrorean, who makes statements that are alternately truthful and false.

Apollo reasons that he needs to find out which one is the Sororean, so he asks that question. The inhabitants don't, however, seem to be very cooperative. Two respond as below, and one of the three doesn't feel like talking:

A.
  1. Neither C nor I are the Midrorean.
  2. B is the Nororean.
  3. B's second statement is true.

B.
  1. I am not the Nororean.
  2. C is the Midrorean.

	A	B	C
1			
2			
3			
Sororean			
Nororean			
Midrorean			

C.   (no response) Which one is the Sororean, which one is the Nororean, and which one is the Midrorean?

Solution on pages 220-221.

SUNFLOWERS GALORE

Hyperborea exists in perpetual springtime. Fields of flowers continually in bloom are enjoyed at all times by the inhabitants. They especially enjoy sunflowers, whose tasty seeds and oil are valuable to all, and they delight in the beautiful sunflower blossoms.

Four inhabitants of the land are discussing the sunflowers and why they are so special. Hyperboreans belong to three groups: Sororeans always speak truthfully, Nororeans always speak falsely, and Midroreans make statements that are alternately truthful and false. To which group or groups do these four speakers belong?

A.   1.   We love to eat sunflower seeds.
           2.   We all belong to the same group.

	A	B	C
1			
2			
3			
Sororean			
Nororean			
Midrorean			

B.   1.   Sunflower oil makes the flowers valuable to us.
       2.   We each belong to a different group.

C.   1.   Sunflower seeds and oil are not valuable to us.
       2.   A's second statement is true.

D.   1.   B's second statement is true.
       2.   A's second statement is also true.
       3.   Sunflowers are overrated;
          they give most of us hay fever.

	A	B	C	D
1				
2				
3				
Sororean				
Nororean				
Midrorean				

Solution on pages 221–222.

WHO'S AN OUTLIER?

In any group of people you can expect to find a few who don't adhere to the conventions accepted by the majority. In this, Hyperboreans are no exception.

There are a few individuals who actually disdain the Hyperboreans' three standards of veracity. They are not Sororeans, who always speak truthfully; Nororeans, who always speak falsely; or Midroreans, who make statements that are alternately truthful and false. They are Hyperborea's Outliers. These inhabitants' statement patterns as to truth and falseness are anything that is different. Therefore, their statements here are, in some order, either two truthful statements in sequence then one false statement, or one truthful statement then two false statements.

Following are statements made by inhabitants, discussing their involvement in the first Olympic Games. One is known to be a Sororean; one is known to be a Nororean; one is known to be a Midrorean; and one is known to be an Outlier. Which is which?

A. 1. B is the Outlier.
    2. I finished in first place in the discus throw.
    3. There is another Olympic Games scheduled for next year.

B. 1. Who's an Outlier? I'm not an Outlier.
    2. A is the Sororean.
    3. A was next to last in the discus throw.

C.   1.   I am the Outlier.
        2.   I entered every event.
        3.   A's third statement is false.

D.   1.   A's first statement is false.
        2.   A's third statement is true.
        3.   C did not enter any of the events.

	A	B	C	D
1				
2				
3				
Sororean				
Nororean				
Midrorean				
Outlier				

Solution on page 222.

APOLLO MEETS AN OUTLIER

The Hyperboreans are favored by Apollo, but he has not had any success in establishing meaningful dialogue with the inhabitants. He is aware that there are those among the Hyperboreans who do not respect their traditional conventions regarding veracity. Perhaps he might have better luck making contact with an Outlier.

Apollo, in disguise, approaches four inhabitants, exactly one of whom is known to be an Outlier, whose standard of veracity is different than that of Sororeans, who always speak truthfully; Nororeans, who always speak falsely; and Midroreans, who make statements that are alternately truthful and false. As to the group or groups of the other three speakers, little is known except that no more than one is a Sororean.

Apollo asks which one of the four is the Outlier. They each respond below:

A. 1. Two of us are Outliers.
    2. B is a Sororean.
    3. B was an Outlier, but he has reformed.
    4. B's third statement is true.

B. 1. I am neither a Nororean nor a Midrorean.
    2. A's first statement is true.
    3. D is a Sororean and C is the Outlier.
    4. A is not the Outlier.

C. 1. D is a Sororean.
    2. I am the Outlier.

3. B's second statement is false.
4. D is neither a Sororean nor a Midrorean.

D. 1. B is either a Midrorean or the Outlier.
2. I am either a Sororean or a Midrorean.
3. C falsely claims to be the Outlier.
4. A's third statement is false.

Apollo throws up his hands in frustration. It is time, he decides, for him to give up and return to Mount Olympus to try to forget about the Hyperboreans.

What group is represented by the each of the four speakers?

	A	B	C	D
1				
2				
3				
4				
Sororean				
Nororean				
Midrorean				
Outlier				

Solution on pages 223–224.

PART III
WORKING WITH
HYPOTHESES

WORKING WITH HYPOTHESES

A hypothetical statement is a statement that has a hypothesis and a conclusion, as in: *If Vanessa is a human, then Vanessa is a living thing.* The hypothesis follows "*If . . .*" In this case, it is ". . . *Vanessa is a human.*" The conclusion follows "*then . . .*" In this case, it is "*Vanessa is a living thing.*"

Is the statement about Vanessa false when the hypothesis is false? That is, would the statement about Vanessa be false when Vanessa was not a human? Suppose that Vanessa is not a human. Then:

    CASE 1—Vanessa may be an animal, such as a rabbit. In
        which case, Vanessa is a living thing.
    CASE 2—Vanessa may be an object, such as a boat. In which
        case, Vanessa is a nonliving thing.

Because Vanessa may be either a living thing or a nonliving thing when Vanessa is not a human, there are no restrictions on the conclusion of the statement. So a false hypothesis does not make a statement false.

Considering CASE 1:

    A. When the hypothesis is false and the conclusion is true, a
        hypothetical statement is true.

Considering CASE 2:

   B. When the hypothesis is false and the conclusion is false, a hypothetical statement is true.

Is the statement about Vanessa true when the hypothesis is true? That is, is the statement about Vanessa true when Vanessa is a human?

      Because Vanessa must be a living thing when Vanessa is a human:

   C. When the hypothesis is true and the conclusion is true, a hypothetical statement is true.

   D. When the hypothesis is true and the conclusion is false— as in: *If Vanessa is a human, then Vanessa is not a living thing*—a hypothetical statement is false.

From this analysis, the following principle emerges: When a hypothetical statement is true, you cannot tell whether the hypothesis is true or whether the conclusion is true; when a hypothetical statement is false, you know immediately that the hypothesis is true and the conclusion is false.

TWO SAGAS

The puzzles in this section contain assumptions that
may or may not be valid. To solve them you must differentiate
between those that are valid and those that are not valid.

THE VOYAGE OF
SINGOOD THE SAILOR

During his growing years, Singood had heard many
tales of his illustrious father, Sinbad the Sailor, and his seven
voyages during which he was able to amass an enormous fortune.
Singood wished to undertake adventures of his own and
achieve fabulous wealth, as did his father.

A GIANT FISH

Singood signed on as a sailor on a merchant ship. After being at sea for several weeks, the ship was blown far off course by a storm and came within sight of what appeared to be an island. The captain and crew, including Singood, attempted to row ashore.

Amazingly, this happened not to be an island but the very same giant fish encountered by Singood's father, Sinbad the Sailor, during the first of his seven voyages at sea. The giant predator's method was to give the appearance of an island in order to engulf any unsuspecting prey that came near. Singood and his fellow sailors sought to escape by swimming back to the ship.

From the statements below, what time of day was it and what was the outcome of the encounter?

1. If the monster fish had just consumed a merchant ship and several whales and was not interested in another meal, then it was evening.
2. If it was morning, the ship and crew were too small to be noticed by the monster.

3. If it was evening, then the monster fish was too old and slow to catch the ship and crew.

4. If the giant fish was too old and slow to catch the crew and ship, then it was morning.

Mark a plus (+) or a minus (−) sign as you determine whether or not a statement is valid.

	too small	too slow	not interested
morning			
evening			

Solution on pages 225–226.

AN ENCHANTED ISLAND

The ship and crew came within sight of an unknown island. The trees and lovely flowers growing on it convinced them that this time it was really an island.

Singood, the first mate, and the second mate went ashore to explore. Unknown to them the island was enchanted, and the instant the three set foot on land they fell under a spell and lost their memories. They could recall nothing, not even who they were or why they were there.

From the statements below, which one of A, B, and C was Singood, which one was the first mate, and which one was the second mate?

1. If A was Singood, then B was the first mate.
2. If B was not Singood, then C was the first mate.
3. If A was the first mate, then B was the second mate.

	1st mate	2nd mate	Singood
A			
B			
C			

As in the previous puzzle, mark a plus or minus sign as you draw your conclusions.

Solution on page 227.

A THIRD ISLAND

Singood decided to take a swim, and the instant he did his memory returned. He called to his shipmates and they were able to return to their ship.

The ship came within sight of another island just as the adventurers were in need of supplies. As they drew near, the sailors beheld a beautiful sight. Wavy palm trees, a glistening waterfall, a crystal clear lake, and many trees laden with ripe fruit could be clearly seen. The captain chose to be cautious and sent Singood, the first mate, and the second mate toward shore in the ship's dinghy.

In spite of Singood's energetic rowing, the island appeared to remain at the same distance as when they had started off. Then, mysteriously, its features began to disappear bit by bit in front of their eyes. Finally, there was nothing left to see but a barren strip of land, which also slowly faded from sight, leaving the sailors with no trace of the land ever having been there.

From the statements that follow, in what order did the principal island features disappear?

1. If the wavy palms vanished first, then the fruit trees vanished third.

2. If the fruit trees vanished third, the waterfall vanished first.

3. If the waterfall vanished first, then the clear lake vanished fourth.

4. If the clear lake vanished fourth, then the fruit trees vanished first.

5. The clear lake vanished first unless either the waterfall or the wavy palms vanished first.

6. If the clear lake vanished first, neither the fruit trees nor the waterfall vanished fourth.

	1st	2nd	3rd	4th
clear lake				
fruit trees				
waterfall				
wavy palms				

Solution on page 227.

RETURN TO THE SHIP

When the three sailors turned back toward their ship, they found it as only a distant speck on the horizon. Realizing that Singood was tired from rowing, they decided to take turns at the task of returning to their ship.

From the statements below, what was the order in which they rowed back to the ship?

1. If Singood was not the first to take a turn rowing, then he was the third to take a turn.
2. If the first mate was first to take a turn rowing, then the second mate was second to take a turn.
3. If the second mate was second to take a turn rowing, then the first mate was third to take a turn.
4. If the first mate was third to take a turn rowing, then Singood was second to take a turn.

	1st mate	2nd mate	Singood
1st turn			
2nd turn			
3rd turn			

Solution on page 228.

A GIGANTIC BIRD

The three sailors rowed their boat toward the ship, but before they were even halfway there, a gigantic bird swooped down on them and plucked them up. They were carried to a distant land, where they were deposited in a nest high in a tree.

From the statements that follow, what was the wingspan of the gigantic bird and how far did it carry the three sailors?

1. If the wingspan of the gigantic bird was either 20 or 30 meters wide, it carried the three sailors for 50 leagues.

2. If the gigantic bird carried the three shipmates 75 leagues, its wingspan was not 40 or 50 meters wide.

3. If the wingspan of the gigantic bird was 40 or 50 meters wide, it carried the three sailors 75 leagues.

4. If the gigantic bird's wingspan was not 40 or 50 meters wide, then it was 20 or 30 meters wide.

	20–30 m.	40–50 m.
50 leagues		
75 leagues		

Solution on page 229.

ATTACKED BY A GIANT SERPENT

After the gigantic bird deposited Singood, the first mate, and the second mate high in a tree, one of the three scrambled to the ground. He was immediately attacked by a giant serpent.

A second of the three hurried to the rescue, and the two sailors managed to discourage the serpent long enough that they were able to retreat safely back into the tree.

Which one of the three sailors was attacked by the serpent, which one came to the rescue, and which one remained in the tree?

1. If Singood was attacked by the serpent, then the first mate stayed in the tree.

2. If the first mate stayed in the tree, the second mate did not go to the rescue.

3. If the second mate did not stay in the tree, the first mate was attacked by the serpent.

4. If Singood stayed in the tree, the first mate went to the rescue.

	attacked	to rescue	stayed
Singood			
1st mate			
2nd mate			

Solution on page 230.

CAPTURED BY THE ONE-EYED GIANT

After the serpent left, the three shipmates began to make their way back to the ship. They hadn't gone far, however, when a storm came up. Seeking refuge in a large cave, they were captured by a manlike creature of enormous size, with only one eye. He deposited them in a corner of the cave, next to a pile of bones. It was apparent that they were to become meals for the giant, if nothing were done.

While the giant slept, blocking the cave entrance with his massive body, the sailors discussed how to escape. Each one had an idea. The three possibilities were: attempt to climb over the giant while he was still sleeping; hide under the pile of bones until the giant left the cave; or sharpen a large stick and stab the giant in the single eye.

From the statements that follow, which shipmate arrived at which idea?

1. If Singood's idea was to stab the giant in the eye, then the second mate's idea was not to hide under the pile of bones.

2.   If the first mate's idea was to stab the giant in the eye, or hide under the bones, then Singood's idea was to climb over the sleeping giant.

3.   If Singood's idea was to climb over the giant, or to hide under the bones, then the first mate's idea was to stab the giant in the eye.

	climb over	stab giant	under bones
Singood			
1st mate			
2nd mate			

Solution on page 231.

ESCAPE FROM THE GIANT

Held captive in the cave by a one-eyed giant, Singood, the first mate, and the second mate considered their options—and did manage to make their escape. The sailors then proceeded on a long journey, which took either two or three months, back to the sea, where they had left their ship.

Which escape idea did they undertake and how long did the return to the sea take?

1.   If the journey took two months, then the three sailors escaped by hiding under a pile of bones.

2.   If the journey took three months, then the sailors escaped from the giant by climbing over him while he was asleep.

3.   If the sailors escaped from the giant by climbing over him while he was asleep, then the journey took two months.

4.   If the sailors did not escape from the giant by stabbing him with a sharpened stick, then the journey took either two or three months.

	climb over	under bones	stab giant
2 months			
3 months			

Solution on page 232.

AN ATTACK BY GIANT SPIDERS

At one point during their long trek to the sea, the three sailors suddenly found themselves under attack by three giant spiders that quickly surrounded them. Taking advantage of the many stones lying about, the sailors quickly began throwing them at the spiders. Each sailor singled out a spider and hurled stones with telling accuracy.

Although the spiders were huge and fierce-looking, with long, menacing-looking legs, they were no match for the three sailors, who found the spider legs to be fragile. One spider suffered a damaged and useless leg from one sailor; the second spider suffered two injured and useless legs by a second sailor; and the third spider suffered three damaged and useless legs from the third sailor's attack. The spiders quickly departed.

Which sailor was able to inflict damage to one spider leg, which to two legs, and which to three legs?

	7 legs	6 legs	5 legs
Singood			
1st mate			
2nd mate			

1.   If the spider with six useful legs was not injured by Singood, then the spider with seven useful legs was injured by Singood.

2.   The spider with seven useful legs was injured by the
      second mate only if the spider with five useful legs was
      injured by Singood.

3.   The spider with six useful legs was not injured by the first
      mate only if the spider with five useful legs was injured
      by Singood.

4.   The spider with seven legs was injured by Singood only if
      the spider with six useful legs was not injured by the first
      mate.

Solution on page 233.

SERPENTMARES !

Considering the terrifying adventures that Singood was experiencing, it is no wonder that he was having nightmares. One night he dreamed that four giant serpents—a red one, a black one, a yellow one, and a green one—attacked the three sailors and each was devoured by one of the serpents. No serpent devoured more than one sailor, and the red serpent definitely had a sailor meal.

In the nightmare, which sailor was devoured by which giant serpent?

1. If the second mate was not devoured by either the blue or green serpent, then the first mate was devoured by the red serpent.

2. The second mate was devoured by the blue serpent, unless the first mate was devoured by the red serpent.

3. If Singood was not devoured by either the black serpent or the blue serpent, then the second mate was devoured by the red serpent.

4. If Singood was devoured by the blue serpent, then the first mate was not devoured by the red serpent

	black	blue	green	red
Singood				
1st mate				
2nd mate				

Solution on page 234.

CONTEST ON THE BEACH

When the three shipmates arrived back at the sea, their ship was nowhere to be seen. There was nothing to do but wait until their ship returned for them or another ship was sighted. During their long wait, to relieve their boredom they decided to have a contest, consisting of three events: a race down the beach, a coconut throw, and a tree climb. Each sailor won one of the three events.

From the statements below, who were the winners of the three events?

1. If the first mate won the race down the beach, then Singood won the coconut throw.

2. If the second mate won the coconut throw, then the first mate won the race.

3. If the second mate won the tree climb, then the first mate won the coconut throw.

4. If the second mate won the race down the beach, then Singood won the tree climb.

5. If Singood won the race down the beach, then the first mate won the tree climb.

	coconut	race	tree climb
Singood			
1st mate			
2nd mate			

Solution on page 235.

THE RESCUE

The sailors waited for rescue for what seemed a long time. Finally, one day, there appeared on the horizon not one but three ships. One ship had three masts and two had four masts. One ship was black, one was green, and one was white. Which one of the three ships rescued the sailors, and how many masts did it have?

1. If the three sailors were not rescued by the white ship, then the rescue ship had four masts.

2. The three sailors were rescued by a black ship, unless it did not have four masts.

3. If the rescue ship was black, then it did not have four masts.

4. If the rescue ship had four masts, then it was green.

5. If the rescue ship had three masts, then it was not white.

	black	green	white
color			
masts			

Solution on page 236.

SIR HECTOR HEROIC
THE DRAGON FIGHTER

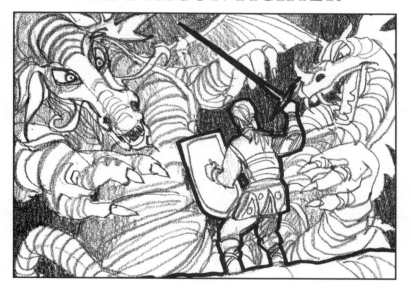

Sir Hector lived in a distant kingdom at a forgotten time.
He and his fellow knights concentrated on adventures
and doing great deeds.

A CONTEST

The dragons in the land had begun to lose their fear and were becoming a serious threat to farm animals, and to vulnerable villagers. The king therefore proclaimed that a contest be held. In one period, sunrise to sunset, knights were to boldly confront as many dragons as they could and either slay them or frighten them so that the dragons would retreat to faraway places. The deemed winner of the contest was to receive a grand prize.

On the eve of the contest, two knights rode deep into the backcountry, where many of the marauding dragons lived, and camped there overnight in order to gain an advantage over other knights.

The winner proved to be either Sir Hector, Sir Able, Sir Bold, or Sir Gallant. From the statements below, who was the contest winner?

1. If Sir Able won the contest, then he concentrated on only the largest dragons in the land.
2. If Sir Hector won the contest, then he did not forget his shield.
3. If Sir Gallant won the contest, then he was the only knight who camped out overnight in the backcountry.
4. Sir Hector was an excellent cook, and during his night in the backcountry, he enjoyed a sumptuous dinner.

5. Sir Able had to quit when his captive mouse, which he kept to attract his prey, escaped.

6. If Sir Hector remembered his shield, then his squire forgot to pack his food.

	Sir Able	Sir Bold	Sir Gallant	Sir Hector
winner				

Indicate a plus or minus as you form your conclusions.

Solution on page 237.

SEEKING ADVENTURE

Craving some excitement, Sir Hector, Sir Able, Sir Bold, and Sir Gallant set out in search of adventure. During their travels, two battled dragons, one battled a giant, and one had a confrontation with a sorcerer.

From the statements below, which knight had which adventure?

1. If Sir Gallant did not confront a sorcerer, then Sir Hector battled a dragon.

2. If Sir Hector did not battle a giant, then Sir Able battled a giant.

3. Sir Bold confronted a sorcerer, if he did not battle a giant.

	dragons	giant	sorcerer
Sir Able			
Sir Bold			
Sir Gallant			
Sir Hector			

Solution on pages 237–238.

THE SWORD-FIGHTING MATCHES

During one tournament, Sir Hector, Sir Able, and Sir Bold were each involved in a sword-fighting match. Two of the knights won their matches and one knight lost. Which two knights won and which knight lost?

1. Sir Able won his match, if Sir Hector lost his match.
2. If Sir Hector won his match, then Sir Bold lost his match.
3. Sir Able lost his match, if Sir Bold won his match.

	Sir Able	Sir Bold	Sir Hector
won			
lost			

Solution on page 238.

MURDER IN THE BLACK CASTLE

It was a dark night, heavy with wind and rain, when three lone knights, strangers to each other, chanced to meet in front of a black and gloomy castle. They were suspicious of each other, but, as was their custom, they approached the castle and sought refuge for the night. The three knights were greeted by a sour-faced servant who explained that the master had retired for the evening but that their needs would be met. The three strangers were then provided food and shown to separate rooms.

	victim	culprit
room 1		
room 2		
room 3		
servant		
master		

Sometime during the night a murder was committed. The crime can be considered somewhat unusual, as not only is the culprit unknown but the identity of the victim is also unclear. Fortunately, the list of possible culprits and victims can be narrowed to five; the servant, the master, and the three knights.

Given the following clues, who was the victim and who was the culprit?

1.   If the knight in room 1 was the culprit, the knight in room 3 was the victim.

2.   If the knight in room 2 was the victim, the servant was the culprit.

3.   If the knight in room 3 was the victim, the knight in room 2 was the culprit.

4.   If the servant was the culprit, the victim was the knight in room 3.

5.   The servant was not available until the next morning, and was not able to provide an alibi.

6.   If the knight in room 3 was the culprit, the knight in room 2 was the victim.

7.   If the knight in room 2 was the culprit, the servant was the victim.

Solution on page 239.

THE MYSTERIOUS MASKED MISCREANT

A mysterious masked miscreant was a thorn in Sir Hector's side. He was a villainous type, guilty of many wrong deeds. Sir Hector finally tracked him down, and the two faced each other, prepared for a fight to the finish. The time of day was morning, early afternoon, or early evening. From the statements that follow, what was the outcome of the confrontation?

1. If Sir Hector pulled off the miscreant's mask and was overwhelmed by the evil face that he saw, then it was morning.

2. If Sir Hector's fellow knights arrived just in time to save him, then it was early afternoon.

3. If it was morning, then Sir Hector had forgotten his sword so didn't stay to do battle.

4. If it was early evening, then Sir Hector's fellow knights arrived just in time to save him.

5. If it was early afternoon, then Sir Hector pulled off the miscreant's mask and was overwhelmed by the evil face that he saw.

	over-whelmed	knights arrived	forgot sword
Sir Hector			
miscreant			

Solution on page 240.

WHO SAW WHICH GIANT?

Most of the giants in the land were peaceful fellows who tended to keep to themselves. However, one lone giant, whose identity is in question, had been taking farm animals at night, causing distress among the farmers. Sir Hector, Sir Able, and Sir Bold offered their help in identifying the culprit, each having seen the thief. Their accounts, though, gave rise to two suspects, giant number one and giant number two.

When a crime has been committed, it's well-known that witnesses often have difficulty recalling what they have seen with any high degree of accuracy. Following are four statements drawn from descriptions of what the three knights claimed to have seen, and assumptions as to the accuracies or inaccuracies of their observations:

1. If giant number one was guilty, then Sir Hector's description was accurate.

2. If Sir Able's description was inaccurate, then giant number two was guilty.

3. If Sir Bold's description was accurate, then Sir Able's description was inaccurate.

4. If Sir Hector's description was accurate, then Sir Bold's description was accurate.

Which of the two giants was guilty?

	giant #1	giant #2
guilty		

Solution on pages 240–241.

SIR HECTOR'S MOST CHALLENGING ADVENTURE

Sir Hector has had many exciting and challenging adventures. When asked which of his past adventures was the most challenging, the brave knight was only able to narrow the list to five. These included the encounter with Grimsby the Giant, the confrontation with the sorcerer, the confrontation with the mysterious masked miscreant, the confrontation with the ancient dragon, and the rescue from the black tower, not necessarily in that order.

From the following statements, can you determine which of Sir Hector's past adventures was the most challenging?

1. If neither the encounter with Grimsby the Giant nor the confrontation with the mysterious masked miscreant was the most challenging adventure, then the confrontation with the ancient dragon was the second most challenging.

2. If the confrontation with the ancient dragon was the second most challenging, then neither the rescue from the black tower nor the confrontation with the sorcerer was the most challenging.

3. If neither the encounter with Grimsby the Giant nor the confrontation with the sorcerer was the second most challenging, then either the confrontation with the mysterious masked miscreant or the confrontation with the ancient dragon was the most challenging.

4.   If the confrontation with the sorcerer was the second
      most challenging, then the rescue from the black tower
      was the most challenging.

	most challenging
dragon	
miscreant	
giant	
tower	
sorcerer	

Solution on pages 241–242.

FOUR FAIR DAMSELS IN DISTRESS

Sir Hector was famous throughout the land for his rescuing of fair damsels in distress. It was said that he had rescued four: Maid Marie, Maid Mary, Maid Morgana, and Maid Matilda. One was rescued from a castle tower where she had been kept by a sorcerer, one from a dragon's lair, one from two giants that were busy fighting over her, and one from the mysterious masked miscreant's hideout.

From the statements below, which fair damsel was rescued from which predicament?

1. If Maid Morgana was not rescued from the miscreant's hideout, then Maid Marie was rescued from a castle tower.

2. Maid Matilda was rescued from the miscreant's hideout, unless Maid Mary found her way home alone from the dragon's lair.

3. If Maid Marie was rescued from a castle tower, then Maid Mary was rescued from two giants.

4. If Maid Matilda was not rescued from the miscreant's hideout, then neither was Maid Morgana.

	2 giants	castle	dragon	miscreant
Maid Marie				
Maid Mary				
Maid Matilda				
Maid Morgana				

Solution on page 242.

ENCOUNTER WITH A GIGANTIC SERPENTLIKE CREATURE

Farmers in the land had sorely complained about a strange, giant, serpentlike creature that was eating livestock, as well as pets and children. Sir Hector, Sir Gallant, and Sir Resolute were determined to confront this gigantic and ferocious beast.

When they encountered the creature, it appeared not nearly as large or ferocious as described. The three decided that one knight should be enough to dispose of this fearful menace. One of the knights went home, one fought the creature, and one stayed to observe. After a short skirmish, the creature agreed to leave for good. The heroic knights later returned to accept the farmers' adulations.

Which knight actually fought the creature, which one stayed to observe, and which one went home?

1. If Sir Gallant did the fighting, then Sir Hector observed.
2. If Sir Hector did the fighting, then Sir Gallant went home.
3. If Sir Gallant went home, then Sir Resolute observed.
4. If Sir Resolute observed, then Sir Gallant did the fighting.
5. If Sir Hector observed, then Sir Resolute did the fighting.

	fought	observed	went home
Sir Hector			
Sir Gallant			
Sir Resolute			

Solution on pages 243.

CONFRONTATION WITH THE GIANT

A giant was taking livestock and terrorizing the people of the land. Sir Hector and his fellow knights, Sir Able, Sir Bold, Sir Gallant, Sir Resolute, and Sir Victor, decided that two of them should confront this giant and drive him from the land. The two adventurers armed themselves and rode to do combat.

When they approached the giant, a short but fierce battle ensued. It was at this point that the giant hap-pened to think of another land, one where he would not encounter so much resistance, and he quickly re-treated, leaving for parts unknown. From the following statements, which two of the knights confronted the giant?

1.   If neither Sir Hector nor Sir Victor confronted the giant, then Sir Gallant did.

	Hector	Able	Bold	Gallant	Resolute	Victor
Hector						
Able						
Bold						
Gallant						
Resolute						
Victor						

2.   If either Sir Gallant or Sir Victor confronted the giant, then Sir Able did not.

3.   If neither Sir Able nor Sir Hector confronted the giant, then Sir Resolute did.

4.   If neither Sir Bold nor Sir Able confronted the giant, then Sir Victor did.

5.   If Sir Hector confronted the giant, then either Sir Gallant or Sir Resolute did.

6.   If Sir Victor was not one of the two who confronted the giant, then neither was Sir Able nor Sir Resolute.

Solution on page 244.

VICTORY AT
THE GRAND TOURNAMENT

Sir Hector, Sir Able, Sir Bold, Sir Gallant, and Sir Resolute each entered the big annual tournament, which attracted knights from all over the land. Two of the five brave knights were victorious over the others, and, since neither would compete against his comrade, they shared the grand prize.

From the statements that follow, which two were victorious?

1.   If Sir Gallant was victorious, then Sir Hector was not victorious.

2.   If Sir Able was victorious, then Sir Gallant was not victorious.

3.   If Sir Hector was not victorious, then Sir Bold was not victorious.

4.   If Sir Resolute was victorious, then Sir Able was victorious.

5.   If Sir Bold was victorious, then Sir Able was not victorious.

6.   Sir Resolute was victorious, if Sir Hector was victorious.

	victorious
Sir Able	
Sir Bold	
Sir Gallant	
Sir Hector	
Sir Resolute	

Solution on page 245.

KNIGHTS' ADVERSARIES

Sir Hector, Sir Able, Sir Bold, and Sir Gallant were each especially skilled at dealing with a certain type of adversary. For one knight it was giant serpents, for one it was dragons, for one it was giants, and for one it was sorcerers.

Based on the following statements, determine which knight was most skilled at dealing with which type of adversary.

1. If Sir Able was the most skilled at dealing with dragons, then Sir Gallant was the most skilled at dealing with giants.

2. If Sir Bold was the most skilled at dealing with giants, then Sir Hector was the most skilled at dealing with sorcerers.

3. If Sir Bold was the most skilled at dealing with sorcerers, then Sir Able was the most skilled at dealing with dragons.

4. If Sir Gallant was not the most skilled at dealing with dragons, then Sir Hector was the most skilled at dealing with giants.

5. If Sir Gallant was the most skilled at dealing with giant serpents, then Sir Bold was not the most skilled at dealing with dragons.

6. If Sir Hector was the most skilled at dealing with sorcerers, then Sir Able was the most skilled at dealing with giants.

7. If Sir Able was the most skilled at dealing with giants, then Sir Gallant was the most skilled at dealing with sorcerers.

	dragons	giants	serpents	sorcerers
Sir Able				
Sir Bold				
Sir Gallant				
Sir Hector				

Solution on page 246.

THREE NOVELS

The puzzles in this section are in the form of three "novels" with each novel consisting of a prologue followed by four chapters. The four chapters are four different puzzles. Three characteristics of the novels are:

(1) The information in the prologue of a novel must be used to solve each chapter of the novel.

(2) The solution to each chapter of a novel is independent of the solutions to the other three chapters.

(3) The kinds of statements in one chapter of a novel are not the same as the kinds of statements in another chapter.

The kinds of statements in a novel occur in the following way:

Chapters 2 and 4 contain false statements, while Chapters 1 and 3 do not.

Chapters 3 and 4 contain hypothetical statements (identified below), while Chapters 1 and 2 do not.

Should you need help, you can refer to a solution scheme that appears at the end of each "novel." Six puzzles involve reasoning with hypothetical statements and three of those puzzles involve deciding which hypothetical statements are true and which are false. See the explanation of hypothetical statements at the beginning of Chapter III.

THE CARD PLAYERS

PROLOGUE

Five adults met regularly to play cards.

[I] The five card players were a widower, his son, his son's wife, his daughter, and his daughter's husband.

[II] Each time they played cards, the chairs in which they sat were arranged this way around a table:

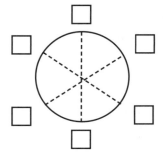

CHAPTER 1: THE SCOREKEEPER

The first time they played cards:

[1] The scorekeeper was the only person who sat between a man and a woman.

[2] Neither woman sat next to her husband.

[3] The oldest man sat next to the empty chair.

Who was the scorekeeper?

Solution Scheme on page 123; Solution on page 247.

CHAPTER 2: THE CHEATER

The third time they played cards, the women tried to get the men to recall the seating arrangement the second time they played cards. The following statements were made in the order given.

[1] Widower: I sat directly across from my daughter.

[2] Widower's son: I sat directly across from my sister's husband.

[3] Widower's daughter's husband: I sat next to the empty chair.

[4] Widower's daughter: Exactly one of you men lied and cheated the second time we played cards.

[5] Widower's son's wife: The man who cheated did not sit next to a woman.

It turned out:

   [6] Each woman told the truth.

      Who was the cheater?

Solution Scheme on page 123; Solution on pages 247–250.

CHAPTER 3 : THE EMPTY CHAIR

The fourth time they played cards, after sitting directly across from the empty chair became a good-luck omen:

   [1] If the widower's son sat directly across from a man, then he sat next to his father.

   [2] If the widower's daughter's husband sat directly across from a man, then he sat next to the widower's son.

   [3] If the widower sat directly across from a woman, then he sat directly across from his daughter.

   [4] If the widower's son's wife sat directly across from a man, then she sat directly across from the widower.

   [5] Each man sat next to a woman.

Who sat directly across from the empty chair?

Solution Scheme on page 124; Solution on pages 251–252.

CHAPTER 4:
DEATH OF A CARD PLAYER

The fifth time they played cards:

[1] The widower was murdered by one of the other four card players.

[2] Each man sat next to a woman.

The next day, because it was thought that the widower was murdered by a person who earlier had sat next to him, the other four card players made the following statements.

[3] Widower's daughter: If only one person sat next to my father, then that person was not me.

[4] Widower's daughter's husband: If only one person sat next to my wife's father, then that person was not me.

[5] Widower's son: If anyone sat directly across from my father, then that person was me.

[6] Widower's son's wife: If anyone sat directly across from my husband's father, then that person was me.

It turned out:

[7] Only the murderer lied.

Who was the murderer?

Solution Scheme on page 124; Solution on pages 252–253.

THE CARD PLAYERS SOLUTION SCHEMES

CHAPTER 1 : THE SCOREKEEPER

Copy the diagram that appears in the Prologue. Using symbols (such as MÓ for the widower, MÔ for the widower's son, WÔ for the widower's daughter, WÒ for the son's wife, MÒ for the daughter's husband, and E for empty), place the players and the empty chair around the table so that no condition is contradicted.

CHAPTER 2 : THE CHEATER

Copy the diagram that appears in the Prologue and make a chart for yourself as follows:

	True	False
Widower's Statement		
Son's Statement		
Daughter's Husband's Statement		

Place the players and the empty chair around the table and put X's in the appropriate boxes of the chart so that the men's statements and the women's statements are consistent with each other and so that [6] is not contradicted.

CHAPTER 3: THE EMPTY CHAIR

Copy the diagram that appears in the Prologue and place the players and the empty chair around the table so that no condition is contradicted. For each of [1] through [4], this means that no conclusion can be false when the hypothesis is true.

CHAPTER 4: DEATH OF A CARD PLAYER

Copy the diagram that appears in the Prologue and make a chart for yourself as follows:

	True	False
Son's Statement		
Daughter's Statement		
Daughter's Husband's Statement		
Son's Wife's Statement		

Place the players and the empty chair around the table and put X's in the appropriate boxes of the chart so that [1], [2], and [7] are not contradicted and so that the suspects' statements are consistent with each other. This means, in chapter, that only one of the suspects' statements can have a false conclusion when the hypothesis is true.

A COMPANY OF ACTORS

PROLOGUE

Five people formed a company of actors.

[I] The actors were three women—Anita, Chloe, and Edith—and two men—Brian and David.

[II] Each of the five actors had a different one of these dressing rooms:

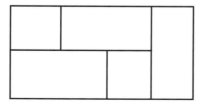

CHAPTER 1 : THE PLAYWRIGHT

For their first play:

[1] The dressing room of the playwright, who was one of the five actors, was the only room that bordered on exactly two other woman-occupied rooms.

[2] Anita's dressing room and Brian's dressing room bordered on the same number of other rooms.

[3] Chloe and David had the same size dressing room.

[4] Edith's dressing room bordered on one more man-occupied room than Anita's did.

Who was the playwright?

Solution Scheme on page 130; Solution on pages 254–255.

CHAPTER 2 : THE WHISTLER

Just before the performance of their second play:

[1]   Reading clockwise from the right end, the dressing rooms were occupied by Edith, Anita, Brian, Chloe, and David.

[2]   One of the five was heard to be whistling—an act puported to be unlucky.

[3]   An investigation turned up evidence that seemed to indicate the whistler had the following characteristics.

    i.   Had a large dressing room.

   ii.   Was a woman.

  iii.   Had a dressing room that bordered on the room occupied by Chloe.

  iv.   Was not David.

   v.   Had a dressing room that bordered on the room occupied by Edith.

 [4] It turned out not to be true that exactly three of these characteristics were correct.

Who was the whistler?

Solution Scheme on page 130; Solution on page 256.

CHAPTER 3 : THE DIRECTOR

During a rehearsal for their third play:

 [1] Reading clockwise from the right end, the dressing rooms were occupied by Anita, Brian, Chloe, Edith, and David.

 [2] The director, who was one of the five actors, revealed that one of the other four was the director's sibling.

 [3] If the director and the director's sibling had dressing rooms that bordered on each other, then the director's sibling was a woman.

[4] If the director and the director's sibling had dressing rooms that bordered on a different number of other rooms, then the director and the director's sibling were the same sex.

[5] If the director and the director's sibling had dressing rooms that were a different size, then the director had a large dressing room.

[6] If the dressing room of the director bordered on a larger number of other rooms than the dressing room of the director's sibling did, then the director and the director's sibling were the opposite sex.

Who was the director?

Solution Scheme on page 131; Solution on pages 257–258.

CHAPTER 4: DEATH OF AN ACTOR

During the performance of their fourth play:

[1] Edith was murdered in her dressing room, which was the small one that bordered on three other rooms.

Many years later, the remaining four actors tried to recall the circumstances surrounding the unsolved murder.

[2] They made the following statements.

Anita: If Edith's dressing room and the murderer's dressing room bordered on the same number of other woman-occupied rooms, then David and I had dressing rooms that were not the same size.

Brian: If Edith's dressing room and the murderer's dressing room did not border on each other, then David and I had dressing rooms that were not the same size.

Chloe: If Edith's dressing room and the murderer's dressing room bordered on each other, then Brian and I had dressing rooms that bordered on each other.

David: If Edith's dressing room and the murderer's dressing room bordered on the same number of other man-occupied rooms, then Brian and I had dressing rooms that were the same size.

It turned out:

[3] Only one person told the truth.

Who was the murderer?

Solution Scheme on page 131; Solution on pages 258–260.

A COMPANY OF ACTORS
SOLUTION SCHEMES

CHAPTER 1: THE PLAYWRIGHT

Copy the diagram that appears in the Prologue and place the actors in the dressing rooms so that no condition is contradicted.

CHAPTER 2: THE WHISTLER

Make a chart for yourself as follows:

	True	False
Characteristic i		
Characteristic ii		
Characteristic iii		
Characteristic iv		
Characteristic v		

Put X's in the appropriate boxes of the chart so that [1], [2], and [4] are not contradicted.

CHAPTER 3 : THE DIRECTOR

Choose a hypothesis, from among [3] through [6], whose truth and then falsehood will produce a minimum of director–sibling pairs that satisfy [1] and [2]. Then use the other three hypotheses from [3] through [6] to eliminate as many of those director–sibling pairs as possible.

CHAPTER 4 : DEATH OF AN ACTOR

Copy the diagram that appears in the Prologue and make a chart for yourself as follows:

	True	False
Anita's Statement		
Brian's Statement		
Chloe's Statement		
David's Statement		

Place the actors in the dressing rooms and put X's in the appropriate boxes of the chart so that [1] and [3] are not contradicted and so that the suspects' statements are consistent with each other. This means, in part, that only three of the suspects' statements can have false conclusions when the hypotheses are true.

THE GOURMET DINERS

PROLOGUE

Some men and women formed a club of gourmet diners
that met for dinner once a month.

[I] The gourmet diners were three women—April, Carla, and
Ellen—and three men—Basil, Derek, and Felix.

[II] At each dinner, the chairs in which they sat were
arranged this way around a table:

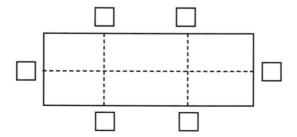

CHAPTER 1:
THE PRESIDENT OF THE CLUB

At the first dinner:

[1]   Each of April and Basil sat on a woman's immediate left.

[2]   Each of Carla and Derek sat on a man's immediate right.

[3]   Each of Ellen and Felix sat directly across from a man.

[4]   The president of the club sat on a woman's immediate left and directly across from a man.

WHO WAS THE PRESIDENT OF THE CLUB?

Solution Scheme on page 136; Solution on pages 260–261.

CHAPTER 2:
THE SUSPECTED POISONER

At the third dinner, when Basil tried to get everyone to recall the seating arrangement at the second dinner, the following statements were made in the order given.

[1]   April: I sat on Basil's immediate right.

[2]   Carla: I sat on a man's immediate left, but it was not Basil's.

[3]   Ellen: I sat on a woman's immediate left.

[4]   Basil: I sat on the immediate right of a woman (he said aloud) who I suspect tried to poison my drink at the second dinner (he said to himself).

[5]   Derek: I sat on the immediate right of a woman who has lied.

[6] Felix: I did not sit next to a woman who has lied.

It turned out:

[7] Each man told the truth.

Whom did Basil suspect of trying to poison his drink?

Solution Scheme on page 136; Solution on pages 261–262.

CHAPTER 3 : THE RECIPE

At the seventh dinner:

[1] Reading clockwise from the right end, the seating arrangement was Ellen, Derek, Basil, April, Felix, and Carla.

[2] One of the six was the cook and another of the six gave the cook the recipe for the dessert.

[3] The cook and the recipe giver did not sit next to each other.

[4] If the cook and the recipe giver sat directly across from each other, then the cook was a woman.

[5] If the cook and the recipe giver were separated by one person, then the recipe giver was a man.

[6] If the cook and the recipe giver were separated by two persons, then the recipe giver was a woman.

[7] If you knew who the recipe giver was at this point, then you would not know who the cook was.

Who was the recipe giver?

Solution Scheme on page 137; Solution on pages 262–263.

CHAPTER 4:
DEATH OF A GOURMET DINER

At the ninth dinner, April was murdered. An investigation of her murder led to a consideration of the following five propositions.

[1] If two women sat directly across from each other, then Basil was the murderer and sat on April's immediate left.

[2] If two men sat directly across from each other, then Carla was the murderer and sat on April's immediate left.

[3] If two women sat next to each other, then Derek was the murderer and sat directly across from April.

[4] If two men sat next to each other, then Ellen was the murderer and sat directly across from April.

[5] If every man sat next to a woman, then Felix was the murderer and sat on April's immediate right.

It turned out:

[6] Only four of the five propositions were true.

Who was the murderer?

Solution Scheme on page 138; Solution on pages 263–265.

THE GOURMET DINERS
SOLUTION SCHEMES

CHAPTER 1:
THE PRESIDENT OF THE CLUB

Copy the diagram that appears in the Prologue and place the diners around the table so that no condition is contradicted.

CHAPTER 2:
THE SUSPECTED POISONER

Copy the diagram that appears in the Prologue and make a chart for yourself as follows:

	True	False
April's Statement		
Carla's Statement		
Ellen's Statement		

Place the diners around the table and put X's in the appropriate boxes of the chart so that [7] is not contradicted and so that the suspects' statements are consistent with each other

CHAPTER 3 : THE RECIPE

Make a chart for yourself as follows:

If the recipe giver was	then the cook could only be

Write a single name in each box so that none of [1] through [6] is contradicted; then use [7].

CHAPTER 4:
DEATH OF A GOURMET DINER

Copy the diagram that appears in the Prologue and make a chart for yourself as follows:

Hypothesis of [1] is		Conclusion of [1] is		[1] is	
Hypothesis of [2] is		Conclusion of [2] is		[2] is	
Hypothesis of [3] is		Conclusion of [3] is		[3] is	
Hypothesis of [4] is		Conclusion of [4] is		[4] is	
Hypothesis of [5] is		Conclusion of [5] is		[5] is	

Write "true" or "false" in each box of the chart and place the diners around the table so that [6] is not contradicted. This means, in part, that only one of [1] through [5] has a false conclusion when its hypothesis is true.

PART IV
COOLING DOWN

COOLING DOWN

This section contains short puzzles that you should be able to solve in a minute or two. Although some are quite tricky, their purpose is to entertain and amuse. When writing is involved, a small slip of paper should be more than adequate. *Solutions on pages 267–277.*

QUICK LOGIC

110

What was the biggest ocean in the world before Balboa discovered the Pacific Ocean?

111

How many cookies could you eat on an empty stomach?

112

Three mature and hefty women were walking in San Francisco under one regular-size umbrella. Why didn't they get wet?

113

What can a pitcher be filled with so it is lighter than when it is full of air?

114

A dog is tied to a 15-foot long leash. How can the dog reach a bone that is 20 feet away?

115

I went into a store and found out that it cost $3 for 400, which meant that each part cost $1. What did I want to buy?

116

Last week, my uncle Peter was able to turn his bedroom light off and get into bed before the room was dark. The light switch and the bed are ten feet apart. How did he accomplish this?

117

How can you make 30 cents with only two coins if one of the coins is not a nickel?

118

The only barber in my town likes foreigners to go into his shop. Last week, he was telling me, "The truth is that I'd rather give two foreigners haircuts than to give a haircut to one person in town." What was the logic behind this?

119

My brother Mark says he is able to place a bottle in the middle of a room and by crawling on the floor, he can slide into it. How can this be?

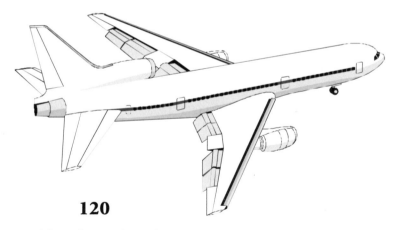

120

Last Friday I flew to San Diego.
It was a scary flight. About an hour after getting onto the plane, I saw a very thick fog and then the engines stopped due to lack of fuel. Why didn't we die?

121

While eating out, my brother-in-law Paul found a fly in his coffee. After taking the cup away, the waiter came back with a different cup of coffee. My brother-in-law got upset and returned it, saying that the coffee in the second cup was the same as in the first one. How did he know?

122

You find shelter in a mountain lodge on a windy night. When you go in, you only find a match, a candle, a sheet of newspaper, and a torch. You need to light the fireplace. What would you light first?

123

A mother has six children and five potatoes. How can she feed each an equal amount of potatoes? (Do not use fractions.)

124

The giraffe and its offspring are walking in a field. The little giraffe tells a friend, "I am the daughter of this giraffe, although this giraffe is not my mother." How can you explain this?

125

A farmer has twenty sheep, ten pigs, and ten cows. If we call the pigs cows, how many cows will he have?

126

Where must a referee be to blow the whistle?

127

In the event of an emergency, can a Muslim baptize a Catholic?

128

It occurs once in a minute, twice in a week, and once in a year. What is it?

129

One night, when my uncle Emil was reading a book in the living room, his wife turned off the light and the living room became completely dark. However, my uncle continued reading. How is this possible?

130

A man says, "I am going to drink water because I don't have water. If I had it, I would drink wine." What does he do for a living?

131

Imagine you are a taxi driver and you are driving a 1978 yellow cab. Your passengers are an older couple, and they want to travel 6 miles. You are driving at 40 miles per hour with the tank one-third full, when, 2 miles into the trip, the tank is down to one-quarter full. Ten minutes later, the trip is over. What is the name and age of the cab driver?

132

A railway line has a double track, except in a tunnel where there was no room for a double track. A train goes into the tunnel in one direction, and another one enters in the opposite direction. Both trains are traveling fast. However, they do not crash. Why?

133

My son was telling me yesterday, "Four days ago, my school's soccer team won a game 4 to 1, although none of the boys on my school's team scored any goals. Also, the other team didn't score against itself accidentally." How can this be?

134

Last Thursday, my aunt Martha forgot her driver's license at home. She was traveling down a one way street in the wrong direction and did not stop at an intersection to let pedestrians go. A policeman was watching her, but did not give her a ticket. Why?

135

Three friends went out for drinks. The waiter brought them a check for $30, so each one of them paid $10. When the waiter took the cash, he realized he had made a mistake, and the check was for $25 instead. When he gave their change back, each friend got a dollar and they left the remaining two dollars as a tip. Therefore, each customer paid $9; multiplied by 3 this equals $27; plus $2 for the tip equals $29. Where is the remaining dollar?

136

A 16-year-old boy was driving a moped down a one-way street in the wrong direction. A policeman stopped him and gave him a ticket. The policeman paid the ticket himself. Can you find a logical explanation for this?

137

The butcher, his daughter, the fisherman, and his wife won the lottery and divided the prize into three. How can this be?

138

My friend Albert the butcher wears a size 13 shoe, is six feet tall, and wears a 42-long suit. What does he weigh?

139

There are five apples in one basket and five people in a room. How can you distribute the apples so that each person receives one and there is one apple left in the basket?

140

A man is doing his work. He knows that if his suit tears, he will die. Can you guess his job?

141

We have just invented two words: to sint and to sant. You cannot sint or sant in the street or in the office. You can do both things in the bathroom, the swimming pool, and the beach, but in the swimming pool and the beach you cannot sint completely. You cannot sint without clothes on and you need little or no clothing to sant. Can you guess what the words mean?

142

My cousin Henry can guess the score of a soccer game before the game begins. How can that be?

143

Before my husband left on a trip, he left me $150 in cash and a $500 check. However, when I went to the bank to cash the check, I found out that the account only had $450. How could I cash the check?

144

A bus stops three times during the ride. The ticket costs 12 cents to the first stop, 21 to the second stop, and 25 to the third stop. A man gets on at the start of the route and gives the driver 25 cents. Without talking to the passenger, the driver gives him a ticket to the last stop. How did the driver know?

146

Mary, riding her white horse, decides to go into the forest. How far can she go?

150

"This parrot can repeat anything it hears," the owner of the pet shop told Janice last week. So my sister bought it. Yesterday, she went to return it, claiming that the parrot had not even said one word. However, the pet shop owner had not lied to her. Can you explain this?

151

A man and his son were in a car accident. The boy had a fracture and injuries to one leg and was taken to a nearby hospital in an ambulance. When he was in the operating room, the surgeon said, "I cannot operate on him! He is my son!" Explain this.

152

Why do black sheep eat less grass than white sheep?

257

Which is warmer, a two-inch thick blanket or two blankets one inch thick each?

258

Three ice cubes are melting in a glass of water. Once they have completely melted, has the water level of the glass changed?

259

A super-accurate bomb, one that always hits the bull's-eye and destroys it, hits an indestructible fort. What will happen?

260

A man gets up 180 times every night and sleeps for at least 7 hours at a stretch. Where does he live?

261

I had just made myself a cup of coffee when I realized I had to run upstairs for a moment. I did not want the coffee to get cold, and I had to add milk at room temperature. Should I add the milk before I go up or after I get back?

LOGIC

153

My cousin Mary dropped an earring in her coffee, but the earring did not get wet. How could this be?

154

I have a book where the foreword comes after the epilogue, the end is in the first half of the book, and the index comes before the introduction. What book is it?

155

How can you explain that one lady works alone as a bartender, yet there is a COUPLE that works behind the counter?

156

My uncle Raphael bought a coin in the flea market for 10 dollars. The coin has the head of Emperor Augustus and is dated 27 b.c. The other side is illegible. It is a fake, however. What proves that it is not a true ancient Roman coin?

157

An Air France plane crashes along the border of Portugal and Spain. Rescue teams from both countries are called to the site of the crash to help the victims. In which country do you think the survivors will be buried?

158

The director of a large company asks the security guard working the night shift to call him a cab, because he needs to take a red-eye flight to New York. The guard tells him not to board the plane, because he had just had a dream that the director would have an accident. To be safe, the director decides to wait until the next morning. During the trip, he reads in the paper that the red-eye flight had crashed. When he returns from his trip, he thanks the guard and gives him a bonus. Then he fires him. Why did he fire him?

159

My cousin Edward got soaked while he was walking on the street yesterday. He did not have an umbrella or a hat, so when he got home, his clothes were completely wet. However, not a hair on his head got wet. Why?

160

My sister Sophie lives on the 28th floor of a 32-story building. When my aunt Emily visits her, she takes the elevator to the 25th floor and then walks up the stairs. On her way down, she takes the elevator at the 28th floor all the way down to the ground floor. Why does she do this?

161

A man was sleeping in a hotel. In the middle of the night, he woke up and could not go back to sleep. He picked up the phone and called someone. As soon as he hung up, he fell sound asleep. He did not know the person he was calling. Why did he call that person?

162

When he goes to the bathroom, a man does not know if the hot water faucet is the one on the left or on the right. What does he need to do to be sure that he does not turn on the cold water before he turns on the hot water?

163

A man took his wife to the emergency room. The doctor decided to operate on her immediately. He told the husband that whether the wife died during the operation or survived, he would charge $1,000. The woman did not survive the operation. The husband did not pay anything. Why not?

164

The brothers Albert, Ben, Carl, and Don wear shirt sizes 37, 38, 39, and 40, respectively. Their mother bought one blue shirt for each one of them and embroidered their first initials on the left side. She placed three initials correctly. How many different ways can this happen?

165

If the date of the last Saturday of last month and the first Sunday of this month do not add up to 33, what month are we in?

166

The priest in my hometown announced last year that on a particular day he would walk on water for half an hour. The river was not dry and we could all see that the priest was actually able to walk on water. How did he manage?

167

Two miners go home after work. One of them has his face covered with soot and the other has a clean face. The one with a clean face wipes it with a handkerchief and the one with the dirty face does not do anything.

Why?

168

What is there in the middle of a cigar?

169

A remote town has two hair salons. The first one has a dirty mirror, a floor covered with hair, and the hairdresser has an awful haircut. In the second one, the mirror and floor are very clean and the hairdresser has a great haircut. Where would you go and why?

170

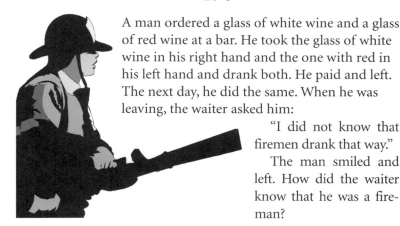

A man ordered a glass of white wine and a glass of red wine at a bar. He took the glass of white wine in his right hand and the one with red in his left hand and drank both. He paid and left. The next day, he did the same. When he was leaving, the waiter asked him:

"I did not know that firemen drank that way."

The man smiled and left. How did the waiter know that he was a fireman?

171

Three meteorologists left a meeting in the middle of the night, during a heavy rain.

"The weather will remain like this until the next full moon," said one of them.

"I agree. And 96 hours from now, the sun will not shine," said the second one.

"I agree more with you than with the first forecast," said the third one.

Why was the third meteorologist so sure?

172

A criminal took his wife to the movies to watch a western. During a gunshot scene he killed his wife with a bullet to her heart. When he left the movies with his wife's dead body, nobody tried to stop him. How did he manage this?

173

In the 5th century A.D. a king was taking his daily bath when he received a huge crown that he had ordered made from one of his bars of gold. He knew that the crown and the gold weighed the same, although he suspected that part of the gold had been replaced with lighter materials, such as copper or silver. How did he find out quickly?

174

If I take two apples out of a basket containing six apples, how many apples do I have?

175

How much will a 38° angle measure when observed under a microscope that magnifies ten times?

176

John Peterson was born in Albany in 1938, on a date not divisible by 2, 3, or 5, and in a month that does not contain the letters "e" or "i." When does he become one year older?

177

A passenger traveling by bus between Springfield and Capital City noticed that due to the heavy traffic, it took him 80 minutes to reach his destination at an average speed of 40 mph. On his return trip, he took the bus and it took him 1 hour and 20 minutes at the same average speed and with less traffic. Do you know why?

178

A man traveling in a taxi is talking to the driver. After a while, the driver tells him, "You must excuse me, but I am deaf and cannot hear a word of what you are saying." The passenger stops talking. After he gets out of the cab, the passenger realizes that the driver had lied to him. How?

182

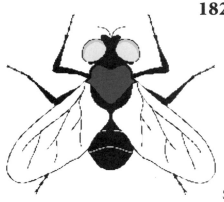

I am sitting at a table. Ten flies are on the table. With one swat, I kill three flies. How many flies are left on the table?

180

A 30-year-old man married a 25-year-old woman. She died at the age of 50 and her husband was so devastated that he cried for years. Ten years after he stopped crying, he died. However, he lived to be 80. How many years was he a widower?

181

Two rich men, now bankrupt, came across each other one day. After exchanging greetings and catching up with what had happened in their lives, they compared how much money each had. The first one had 80 dollars and the second one had only 42 dollars. However, two hours later, between both of them they had more than 84 million dollars in cash. None of them had inherited anything, won the lottery, or received payment for a debt or loan. How could this be?

262

A raft loaded with rocks is floating in a swimming pool. We mark the level of water in the swimming pool and on the raft. If we drop the rocks into the pool, what will happen to the water level in the pool and to the flotation line of the raft? Will they go up or down?

264

Two ivy branches sprout out of a tree trunk from the same point at ground level. One wraps around four times to the right, the other wraps around five times to the left, and their ends meet. Without counting the ends, how many times do both branches of ivy intersect?

265

An African trader is visiting different tribes in a raft loaded with sacks of salt, which he trades according to their weight in gold.

When he is about to trade them, he realizes that the scale is broken. How can he trade the same weight of salt for gold?

TIME

69

A schoolteacher uses a five-hour hourglass to keep track of class time. One day, he sets the hourglass at 9 a.m. and while he is teaching his class, a student inadvertently inverts the hourglass. Another student, who notices this, sets the hourglass to its initial position at 11:30 a.m. In this way, the class ends at 3 p.m. At what time did the first student invert the hourglass?

70

A clock gains half a minute every day. Another clock doesn't work. Which one will show the correct time more often?

72

In a conventional clock, how many times does the minute hand pass the hour hand between noon and midnight?

73

If a clock takes two seconds to strike 2, how long will it take to strike 3?

74

When I gave Albert a ride home, I noticed that the clock in his living room took 7 seconds to strike 8. I immediately asked him, "How long do I have to wait to hear it strike 12?"

75

A clock takes five seconds when striking 6. How long will it take when striking 12?

38

A spider spins its web in a window frame. Each day, it spins an area equal to that of the amount already completed. It takes 30 days to cover the entire window frame. How long would two spiders take? (In the case of two spiders, each of them spins an amount equal to the area of the existing part of the web made by that particular spider.)

77

On March 15, a friend was telling me, "Every day I have a cup of coffee. I drank 31 cups in January, 28 in February and 15 in March. So far, I drank 74 cups of coffee. Do you know how many cups I would have drunk thus far if it had been a leap year?"

78

If yesterday had been Wednesday's tomorrow and tomorrow is Sunday's yesterday, what day would today be?

79

Mrs. Smith left on a trip the day after the day before yesterday and she will be back the eve of the day after tomorrow. How many days is she away?

80

A man was telling me on a particular occasion, "The day before yesterday I was 35 years old and next year I will turn 38." How can this be?

81

A famous composer blew out 18 candles on his birthday cake and then died less than nine months later. He was 76 at the time of his death and had composed The Barber of Seville. How could this happen?

WORDS

83

If you can speak properly, you will be able to answer the following question. Which is correct, "The yolk of an egg is white" or "The yolk of an egg are white"?

84

What is the opposite of

"I AM NOT LEAVING"?

85

What 11-letter word is pronounced incorrectly by more than 99% of Ivy League graduates?

86

What 7-letter word becomes longer when the third letter is removed?

87

Five times four twenty, plus two, equals twenty-three. Is this true?

88

Paris starts with an "p" and ends with an "e." Is this true?

89

A phone conversation:

"May I speak to the director?"

"Who's calling?"

"John Rominch."

"I beg your pardon. Could you spell your last name?"

"R as in Rome, O as in Oslo, M as in Madrid, I as in Innsbruck ..."

"I as in what?"

"Innsbruck."

"Thanks. Please go ahead."

"N as in Nome ..."

This does not make sense. Why?

90

What can you always find in the middle of a taxicab?

91

Is the sentence "This statement is false" true or false?

92

What occurs once in June and twice in August, but never occurs in October?

93

"I must admit that I was not serious when I was telling you that I was not kidding about rethinking my decision of not changing my mind," my friend was telling me. So, is he really going to change his mind or not?

94

A criminal is sentenced to death. Before his execution, he is allowed to make a statement. If his statement is false, he will be hanged, and if his statement is true, he will be drowned. What should he say to confuse the jury and thus save his life?

FAMILY TIES

95

A woman has five children and half of them are male. Is this possible?

96

A friend was telling me, "I have eight sons and each has one sister." In total, how many children does my friend have?

97

Ann's brother has one more brother than sisters. How many more brothers than sisters does Ann have?

98

"I have as many brothers as sisters, but my brothers have twice the number of sisters as brothers. How many of us are there?"

99

A doctor has a brother who is an attorney in Alabama, but the attorney in Alabama does not have a brother who is a doctor. How can this be?

100

John wonders, "If Raymond's son is my son's father, how am I related to Raymond?"

101

If your uncle's sister is related to you, but is not your aunt, what is the relation?

102

A group of paleontologists found a prehistoric cave and one of them is congratulated by a younger son, who writes a telegram to his dad explaining the discovery. Who discovered the cave?

103

The other day, I heard the following conversation:

"Charles is related to you the same way I am to your son."

"And you are related to me in the same way Charles is to you."

How are Charles and the second man related?

104

Can someone marry his brother's wife's mother-in-law?

105

Ann is looking at the portrait of a gentleman. "He is not my father, but his mother was my mother's mother-in-law," she says. Who is this gentleman?

106

Do you know if the Catholic Church allows a man to marry his widow's sister?

109

Two women are talking on the street. When they see two men coming, they say, "There are our fathers, our mothers' husbands, our children's fathers, and our own husbands." How can you explain this?

LAUGHS

273

My cousin Henry can predict the future when he pets his black poodle. Is that possible?

274

An older woman and her young daughter, a young man, and an older man are traveling in the same compartment of a train. When the train passes through a tunnel, they hear a kiss and a slap. As the lights come back on, they can see the older man with a black eye. This is what each of the passengers thought:

The older woman: "He deserved it. I am glad my daughter can defend herself."

The daughter: "I cannot believe he pre-ferred to kiss my mother or that young man over kissing me."

The older man: "What is going on here? I didn't do anything! Maybe the young man tried to kiss the girl, and she mistakenly slapped me."

The young man: "I know what really happened."

Do you know what happened?

275

An electric train runs at 60 mph heading south toward a wind blowing at 30 mph. What is the direction of the smoke from the train?

276

If Albert's peacock jumps over the fence onto Edward's property and lays an egg there, whose egg is it?

277

What can you have in an empty pocket? (Apart from air, of course.)

278

What did the twelve apostles make?

279

My cousin Herbert told me yesterday, "I can easily bite my eye." How can this be?

280

It sings and has ten feet. What is it?

281

Mary married John two years ago. She did not bring any money into the marriage and did not work during these two years, but she made her husband a millionaire. How did she do it?

282

My cousin Herbert told me this morning, "I can easily bite my good eye." How can he do this?

283

What can elephants make that no other animal can?

284

Last Thursday I walked back home from work (2 miles), and noticed a strange man following me the entire way. Once I got home, the man was still there walking around my building (a 100-by-100-yard square building). Later on, I saw he had fallen asleep next to the street lamp at the entrance of my building. During which lap did he fall asleep?

285

How can you get into your home if there is a dangerous dog inside that doesn't know you and belongs to your wife's friend?

286

A turtle, a gopher, and a hare are walking one behind the other in a straight line.

"I am first," said the turtle.

"I am second," said the gopher.

"I am first," said the hare.

How can you explain these statements?

287

What activity can only be done at night?

288

My cousin Robert was pushed into a well measuring six feet in diameter and 10 feet deep, with smooth walls and its bottom covered with water. How did he emerge from the well?

289

Every day, a cyclist crosses the border between Spain and France carrying a bag. No matter how much customs officials investigate him, they do not know what he is smuggling. Do you?

SOLUTIONS

PART I.
WARMING UP

THE A'S

FOUR VEHICLES

∾ **Considerations**—From statement 1, Mr. Terrill drives a white vehicle, which is not the sedan. From statements 2 and 5, Mrs. Terrill drives the pickup truck, which is red. From statement 3, the vehicle Johnny drives to school is not the roadster, and from statement 4, since the two vehicles remaining for Johnny are the sedan and the sports utility vehicle, he drives the sports utility vehicle. (The sports utility vehicle is brand new.) It is yellow. The antique vehicle is the sedan; it is green.

∾ **Summary Solutions**—

Mr. Terrill	white roadster
Mrs. Terrill	red truck
Johnny	yellow sports utility vehicle
extra car	green sedan

HALLOWEEN COSTUMES

∿ **Considerations**—From statements 1 and 5, Jimmy and Molly are the Dixons. From statements 2 and 3, Billy is not Smith. Therefore, he is Finley. Therefore, Sam is Smith.

From statements 1 and 2, it was Billy Finley who wore the witch costume. Therefore, Sam wore the pirate costume. From statements 1 and 4, Jimmy wore the skeleton costume, and Molly wore the Robin Hood costume.

∿ **Summary Solutions**—

Billy Finley	witch costume
Jimmy Dixon	skeleton costume
Molly Dixon	Robin Hood costume
Sam Smith	pirate costume

GOLFING COUPLES

∿ **Considerations**—The average score of the four players was 93.5 strokes (187 divided by 2). Therefore, from statement 3, one of the Alberts scored 93 and the other scored 94. From statement 4, the average score of the two men was 94.5 and the average score of the two women was 92.5.

From statement 2, Kathryn's score must have been 94, and Carol's score was 91. Therefore, Kathryn's married name was Albert and, from statement 1, she was married to George, who scored 93 points. Carol Baker was married to Harry, who scored 96 points.

≈ Summary Solutions—

Carol Baker	91 points
George Albert	93 points
Harry Baker	96 points
Kathryn Albert	94 points

VACATION TRIPS

≈ Considerations—From statements 1, 2, and 3, Joyce's husband is not Jack or John. Therefore, it is James. From statements 3 and 4, their surname is Adams. From statement 1, they are going to Atlanta.

From statement 5, Joan is not Abernathy. Therefore, her surname is Anderson. From statements 2 and 3, her husband is John. Their destination is Santa Barbara. Therefore, Jean and Jack Abernathy's destination is Tucson.

≈ Summary Solutions—

Jack and Jean	Abernathy	Tucson
James and Joyce	Adams	Atlanta
John and Joan	Anderson	Santa Barbara

ACCOMPLISHED SISTERS

∾ **Considerations**—From statements 1 and 2, the sister who plays the clarinet speaks Italian, and the one who speaks Spanish plays the piano. From statement 3, Sheri must be the sister who speaks French, and she plays either the violin or the flute. From statements 4 and 5, Ellen speaks Spanish and plays the piano, and Renee must be the sister who plays the clarinet and speaks Italian. Therefore, it is Theresa who plays the violin and speaks German, and Sheri plays the flute.

∾ **Summary Solutions**—

Ellen	piano	Spanish
Renee	clarinet	Italian
Sheri	flute	French
Theresa	violin	German

SUMMER FUN

⌇ **Considerations**—From statements 3 and 5, Theresa and Tony were playing catch. From statement 4, Tony is not 6, and from statement 3, Tony is one of the two five-year-olds. From statements 1 and 5, Theresa is the seven-year-old. From statements 1 and 5, Ted was playing with a dog. Therefore, Timmy was flying a kite. From statement 5, Ted, who is not older than Timmy, must be the other five-year-old, and Timmy is the six-year-old.

⌇ **Summary Solutions**—

Ted	5 years old	playing with dog
Timmy	6 years old	kiting
Theresa	7 years old	playing catch
Tony	5 years old	playing catch

THE B'S

THE MIDVILLE MUDDLERS

∾ **Considerations**—From statement 6, Henry must be the center fielder. However, the indication that his batting average is lower than that of the catcher cannot be correct, considering statement 1. Statements 3 and 5 are also contradictory to statement 6. Therefore, statement 6 is false.

From statements 1 and 3, since Leo is not the catcher, he is the center fielder who bats .295. From statements 2 and 4, Leo must be one of the three players who are neighbors. Therefore Leo's surname is Clements. From statements 1 and 4, Ken, whose batting average is 30 points below Stan's, is the catcher, whose batting average is .280; Stan's batting average is .310. From statements 2 and 5, Stan's surname is Brooks, and he is the right fielder.

From statement 5, Henry's surname is not Ashley. Therefore, Henry is Dodson, the left fielder, whose batting average is .325. Ken's surname is Ashley.

∾ **Summary Solutions**—

Henry Dodson	left fielder	.325
Ken Ashley	catcher	.280
Leo Clements	center fielder	.295
Stan Brooks	right fielder	.310

FISHING VACATION PLANS

∿ **Considerations**—From statements 1, 3, 6, and 7, Barrott's first name is neither Andy, Bill, Carl, nor Dennis. Therefore, one of these four statements is the false one. From statement 5, Barrott was one of the two who are not married. This is contradictory to statement 3. Therefore, statement 3 is false.

Therefore, Barrott's first name is Carl. From statements 4 and 6, Dennis is not Whelan or Crowley. Therefore, Dennis is Cole.

From statements 4, 6, and 7, Whelan's favorite destination was the third, Crowley's was the last, and Barrott's was the first. Therefore, Cole's favorite destination was the second one.

Our conclusions so far are:

From statement 4, the third destination was neither Patagonia nor New Zealand. Therefore, it was either Alaska or Iceland. From statement 6, the trip to New Zealand was not planned to be the first or the fourth destination. From statement 2, the trip to Iceland was planned for the year before the trip to Alaska. Therefore, the first trip must have been planned for Patagonia; the second trip, New Zealand; the third trip, Iceland; and the fourth trip, Alaska.

From statement 2, Andy's favorite destination was not Alaska (which, from statement 6, was Crowley's favorite). Therefore, Andy is Whelan and Bill is Crowley.

∿ **Summary Solutions**—

Andy Whelan	Iceland	third
Bill Crowley	Alaska	fourth
Carl Barrott	Patagonia	first
Dennis Cole	New Zealand	second

WHITEWATER RAFTING

〜 **Considerations**—From statement 5, Henry and Hughes were on the same raft. However, this is inconsistent with statement 7, which states that Alan and Hughes were on the same raft. One of these two statements is false. Statement 7, which states that they were the first to finish, is inconsistent with statement 10, which indicates that they were last. Therefore, statement 7 is the false one.

From statement 6, Hawley was with Frank on the second-place yellow raft. From statements 2, 4, 6, and 10, Paul and Alan Wilson were on the third-place blue raft. From statement 1, Phil and Cook must be on the yellow raft, so they must be Phil Hawley and Frank Cook. From statements 2 and 5, Walt (who was not on the red raft) was on the green raft. From statements 2, 5, and 9, the partners on the red raft were Henry Gladstone and Don Hughes. From statements 3 and 8, the two on the green raft must have been LeRoy Sands and Walt Smith. O'Brien is Paul's surname.

〜 **Summary Solutions**—

Alan Wilson / Paul O'Brien	blue raft	3rd place
Phil Hawley / Frank Cook	yellow raft	2nd place
Walt Smith / LeRoy Sands	green raft	1st place
Henry Gladstone / Don Hughes	red raft	did not finish

SPELLING CONTEST

~ **Considerations**—From statements 6 and 7, Helen is not Knudson or Olsen, and from statement 1, she is not North. Therefore, Helen is Salisbury. From statement 4, Eric placed second. Therefore, from statement 6, he is not Knudson. From statement 4, Eric is not Olsen. Therefore, Eric is North. From statement 5, Gordie did not win, but placed higher than Jennings. Therefore, since Knudson placed fifth (statement 6), Gordie is Olsen and Lois is Knudson. Eleanor Jennings placed fourth, Gordie Olsen placed third, and Eric North placed second (statement 5). Helen Salisbury was the winner.

From statements 1 and 2, Lois misspelled "physiognomy," Eleanor misspelled "bivouac," Gordie misspelled "vicissitude," and Eric misspelled "isthmus."

~ **Summary Solutions**—

Eleanor Jennings	bivouac	4th place
Eric North	isthmus	2nd place
Gordie Olsen	vicissitude	3rd place
Helen Salisbury		1st place (winner)
Lois Knudson	physiognomy	5th place

AUDUBON FIELD TRIP

∾ **Considerations**—From statement 5, Curtis's spouse is an active Audubon member. From statement 3, Curtis's spouse is not Rosemary or Nancy. However, from statement 7, Nancy's husband is Curtis. Either statement 3, 5, or 7 is false. Statement 7 is also inconsistent with statement 10. Therefore, statement 7 is false. From statements 5 and 6, Angela is not married to Curtis. Therefore, Curtis's spouse is Susan (statements 3 and 5).

From statement 8, a pine siskin and a yellow warbler were sighted by the Dwyers. From statement 6, a lazuli bunting was sighted by Angela, and from statement 3, neither Rosemary nor Nancy is Dwyer. Therefore, Susan and Curtis are the Dwyers. From statement 10, Curtis was the last to sight his bird. Therefore, since the pine siskin was sighted early in the day (statement 8), it was sighted by Susan, and Curtis sighted the yellow warbler.

From statements 1 and 2, neither James nor William, who sighted a golden-crowned kinglet, is Brinkley. Therefore, Harold, who sighted a white-crowned sparrow (from statement 9), is Brinkley. From statement 3, neither Rosemary nor Nancy is Valentine. Therefore, Angela is Valentine. Since, from statement 1, James is not Valentine, William is Valentine and Angela's spouse. Therefore, James must be Eng. From statement 9, Nancy, who is not Harold Brinkley's spouse, must be the spouse of James Eng. Rosemary's spouse is Harold.

From statements 4 and 9, Nancy was not the first to sight a western tanager or a black-headed grosbeak. Therefore, she was first to sight an acorn woodpecker. Since, from statement 1, James was not the first to sight a western tanager, he was the first to sight a black-headed grosbeak. Rosemary was the first to spot a western tanager.

∾ Summary Solutions—

Angela Valentine	lazuli bunting
William Valentine	golden-crowned kinglet
Curtis Dwyer	yellow warbler
Susan Dwyer	pine siskin
Harold Brinkley	white-crowned sparrow
Rosemary Brinkley	western tanager
James Eng	black-headed grosbeak
Nancy Eng	acorn woodpecker

CAR POOL

∾ **Considerations**—From statement 1, Amarol must be one of the three women. This, however, is inconsistent with statement 7. Also, from statement 1, Amarol is the first to be dropped off in the evening. This is inconsistent with both statements 3 and 6. Therefore, statement 1 is false.

From statement 2, neither Neal nor Florence is the secretary. From statements 3 and 4, since the secretary is the second to be picked up in the morning, Paul, who is the sixth to be picked up in the morning, is not the secretary. From statement 6, since

Gloria is dropped off immediately after Avenal, who is dropped off first (statement 3), she is dropped off second, and Evelyn, who is dropped off two people later, is the fourth to be dropped off in the evening. Since the secretary is the fifth to be dropped off in the evening (statement 4), neither Gloria nor Evelyn is the secretary. Therefore, Milton, the secretary, is the second to be picked up in the morning and the fifth to be dropped off in the evening.

From statement 7, Avenal and Amarol are two of the three men. Since Paul is not Avenal (statement 3), and, from statement 6, Amarol is the third to be dropped off (immediately before Evelyn, who is the fourth to be dropped off), Milton is not Amarol. Therefore, Paul is Amarol, and Neal is Avenal, the first to be dropped off. Therefore, Florence is Adams the attorney, who is the first to be picked up in the morning and the sixth to be dropped off in the evening (statement 5). From statement 6, Gloria, who is picked up immediately after Neal and before Paul, is the fifth to be picked up, and Neal is the fourth to be picked up in the morning. Therefore, Evelyn is the 3rd to be picked up in the morning.

From statement 2, the secretary (who is Milton) is neither Agassi nor Atwater. Therefore, Milton is Altchech. From statement 4, Paul Amarol, who is the third to be dropped off in the evening, is the word processing supervisor. From statement 8, the personnel manager, who is not the fourth or fifth to be picked up in the morning, is Evelyn; since she is not Atwater, she is Agassi, and Gloria is Atwater. From statement 7, since Neal Avenal is not the systems analyst, he is the computer programmer, and Gloria Atwater is the systems analyst.

∾ Summary Solutions—

carpoolers	positions	a.m. pickup	p.m. drop-off
Evelyn Agassi	personnel manager	3rd	4th
Florence Adams	attorney	1st	6th
Gloria Atwater	systems analyst	5th	2nd
Milton Altchech	secretary programmer	2nd	5th
Neal Avenal	computer	4th	1st
Paul Amarol	word processing supervisor	6th	3rd

THE C'S

CLOUD FORMATIONS

〰 **Considerations**—Only one statement is true.

Assume that statement 1 is the true statement. If so, since Charlie did not see an alligator or a rabbit, those two animals must have been seen by two of Andy, Becky, and Diane. If so, from statement 3, which would be false, Becky saw a flock of sheep. From statement 4, which would be false, neither Andy nor Diane spotted an alligator. Therefore, statement 1 is not the true statement.

Assume statement 3 is true. If so, Becky did not spot the flock of sheep. If not, the flock of sheep was spotted by Charley, Diane, or Andy. From statement 1, which we know to be false, Charlie spotted an alligator or a rabbit; and from statement 4, which would be false, neither Andy nor Diane spotted a flock of sheep. Therefore, statement 3 is false.

Assume statement 4 is the true one. If so, Andy's and Diane's cloud formations were an alligator and a flock of sheep, in some order. If so, the lion and the rabbit must have been seen by Becky and Charlie. However, from statement 2, which would be false, Charlie did not spot the lion, and from statement 3, Becky saw the flock of sheep. Therefore, statement 4 is false.

Therefore, statement 2 is the true statement. Either Diane or Charlie saw a lion. From statement 1, Charlie saw either an alligator or a rabbit. Therefore, Diane saw the lion. From statement 3,

Becky spotted the flock of sheep. From statement 4, Andy did not spot the alligator. Therefore, he spotted the rabbit, and Charlie spotted the alligator.

FOUR VOCATIONS

∿ **Considerations**—Only one statement is true.

Assume that statement 1 is the one true clue. If so, Mr. Carpenter is the baker. If so, from statement 4, Mr. Cook is not the carpenter. Therefore, he must be the butcher. However, from statement 3, the butcher must be Mr. Baker. Therefore, statement 1 is false.

Assume that statement 3 is true. If so, since the butcher is neither Mr. Baker nor Mr. Carpenter, Mr. Cook must be the butcher. If so, from statement 1, Mr. Carpenter is not the baker, and from statement 2, the cook must be either Mr. Butcher or Mr. Baker. Therefore, that leaves Mr. Carpenter with the vocation of carpenter—not possible. Therefore, statement 3 is false.

Assume statement 4 is true. If so, Mr. Cook is the carpenter. If so, from statement 1, Mr. Carpenter is not the baker, and from statement 2, the cook must be either Mr. Butcher or Mr. Baker. Therefore, Mr. Carpenter must be the butcher. From statement 5, Mr. Butcher is not the baker, and therefore must be the cook, which leaves Mr. Baker as the baker—not possible. Therefore, statement 4 is false.

Assume statement 5 is true. If so, Mr. Butcher is the baker. If so, from statement 2, Mr. Carpenter is not the cook. Therefore, he must be the butcher. From statement 4, Mr. Cook is not the carpenter, which leaves him the remaining vocation, cook—not possible. Therefore, statement 5 is false.

Therefore, statement 2 is the true one. Mr. Carpenter is the cook. From statement 3, Mr. Baker is the butcher. From statement 5, Mr. Butcher, who is not the baker, is the carpenter, and Mr. Cook is the baker.

∿ Summary Solutions—

Mr. Baker	butcher
Mr. Butcher	carpenter
Mr. Cook	baker
Mr. Carpenter	cook

FRIENDS AND CATS

∿ **Considerations**—Only one statement is true.

Assume that statement 2 is true. If so, Betsy's cat is named Alice. If so, Dody's cat must be named Betsy or Candy. However, from statement 3, which would be false, Dody does not own either Candy or Betsy. Therefore, statement 2 is false; Betsy's cat is named either Dody or Candy.

Assume statement 3 is the true statement. If so, Dody's cat is named Candy or Betsy. From statement 1, which is false, Candy's cat must be Betsy, so Dody's is Candy. If so, Alice's cat must be named Dody. However, from statement 4, which would be false, Alice's cat is named Betsy or Candy. Therefore, statement 3 is false; Dody's cat is not named Candy or Betsy. Her cat must be named Alice.

Assume that statement 4 is the true statement. If so, Alice's cat is not named Betsy or Candy. If not, Alice's cat must be named Dody. However, from statement 5, which would be false, the cat named Dody belongs to either Candy or Betsy. Therefore, statement 4 is false; Alice's cat is named Betsy or Candy.

Assume that statement 5 is the true statement. If so, the cat named Dody does not belong to Candy or Betsy. If not, the cat named Dody must belong to Alice. However, from statement 4, which is false, Alice's cat is either Betsy or Candy.

Therefore, statement 1 is the true statement. Candy owns Dody or Alice. We know from statement 3, which is false, that Dody's cat is named Alice. Therefore, Candy's cat is Dody. From statement 2, which is false, we know that Betsy's cat is named Dody or Candy. Therefore, Betsy's cat is named Candy. Therefore, Alice's cat is named Betsy.

∾ **Summary Solutions—**

   Alice's cat is Betsy.

   Betsy's cat is Candy.

   Candy's cat is Dody.

   Dody's cat is Alice.

THE MOUNTAINTOP HERMITS

~ **Considerations**—Only one statement is true.

Assume that statement 2 is the true statement. If so, the brothers' summer meetings must have been either at the shelter that faced east or the shelter that faced west. If so, from statement 4, which would be false, their summer meetings must have been at either Homer's or Billy's shelter. However, from statement 3, which would be false, neither Homer's nor Billy's shelters faced east or west. Therefore, statement 2 is false.

Assume that statement 3 is true. If so, the shelters of Billy and Homer faced east and west, in some order. However, from statement 1, which would be false, Billy's shelter faced south. Therefore, statement 3 is false.

Assume that statement 4 is the true one. If so, their summer meetings were either at Jacob's or Willy's shelter. However, from statement 2, which is false, their summer meetings were at either the shelter that faced north or the one that faced east. From statement 3, which is false, neither Billy nor Homer lived in a shelter facing north or south. Therefore, Jacob and Willy lived in shelters that faced north and south, in some order. Therefore, statement 4 is false.

Assume that statement 5 is the true one. If so, Jacob's shelter faced south. However, from statement 3, which we know to be false, Jacob lived in a shelter facing east or west. Therefore, statement 5 is false.

Therefore, statement 1 is the true statement. From statement 1 (true) and statement 3 (false), Billy's shelter faced north, and

Homer's shelter faced south. Homer hosted the spring meeting. From statement 4 (false), Billy hosted the summer meeting.

From statement 5 (false), Jacob hosted the winter meeting. Therefore, Willy hosted the fall meeting. From statement 4 (false), Willy's shelter faced east. Therefore, Jacob faced west.

∿ Summary Solutions—

Billy	north	summer
Homer	south	spring
Jacob	west	winter
Willy	east	fall

SAILBOAT RACE

∿ **Considerations**—Only one statement is true.

Assume that statement 1 is the true statement. If so, the Steinbergs must have finished in fourth or fifth place. From statement 6, which would be false, the Steinbergs must have finished ahead of the Stahls, so must have finished in fourth place, and the Stahls finished in fifth place. However, from statement 5, which would be false, the Stanfords must have finished in fourth or fifth place. Therefore, the Stein-bergs did not finish in fourth place. Therefore, statement 1 is false; the Steinbergs were either one of the two couples who tied for first place or the couple who finished in third place.

Assume that statement 2 is true. If so, the Stanfords finished in third place. However, from statement 5, which would be false, the Stanfords must have finished in fourth or fifth place. Therefore, statement 2 is false; the Stanfords did not finish in third place.

Assume that statement 3 is the true statement. If so, the Stewarts finished ahead of the Smiths and behind the Stanfords. If so, from statement 5, which would be false, the Stanfords must have finished in fourth place and the Stewarts in fifth place. However, this leaves no place for the Smiths. Therefore, statement 3 is false; the Stewarts finished ahead of the Stanfords and behind the Smiths.

Assume that statement 5 is true. If so, the Stanfords did not finish in either fourth place or fifth place. However, from statement 2, which is false, the Stanfords did not finish in third place; and from what we know from statement 3, the Stewarts finished ahead of the Stanfords and behind the Smiths. Therefore, statement 5 is false.

Assume that statement 6 is true. If so, the Stahls finished ahead of the Steinbergs and the Smiths. However, from statement 3, which we know is false, the Stanfords must have finished behind both the Stewarts and the Smiths. However, the two who tied for first place must have been two of the Steinbergs, the Smiths, and the Stahls. Therefore, the Stahls could not have finished ahead of both. Therefore, statement 6 is false.

So statement 4 is the true statement. The Smiths finished in third place and the Stanfords in fifth place. The Stewarts were in fourth place, and the Steinbergs and Stahls tied for first place.

∾ **Summary Solutions—**

lst place	**Steinbergs and Stahls (tied)**
3rd place	**Smiths**
4th place	**Stewarts**
5th place	**Stanfords**

JAZZ COMBO

∾ **Considerations**—Only one statement is true.

Assume statement 1 is true. If so, Caroline is the tenor sax player. From statement 6, which would be false, Roger or Al plays the sax. Therefore, statement 1 is false; Caroline doesn't play the sax.

Assume that statement 2 is true. If so, Steve does not play the piano or the bass. If not, he must play the drums, the guitar, or the sax. From statement 3, which would be false, Steve is not the guitar player. From statement 6, Steve doesn't play the sax. From statement 7, Steve doesn't play the drums. Therefore, statement 2 is false.

Assume statement 4 is the true one. If so, Ansel does not play the guitar, piano, or bass. If not, he must play the sax or the drums. From statement 6, which would be false, he doesn't play the sax, and from statement 7, he doesn't play the drums. Therefore, statement 4 is not the true statement.

Assume statement 5 is the true statement. If so, the drums are not played by Caroline, Ansel, or Roger. If not, the drums are played by Steve or Al. From statement 7, which would be false, the drums are not played by Steve or Al. Therefore, statement 5 is false.

Assume that statement 6 is the true statement. If so, the sax is not played by Roger or Al. If not, the sax must be played by Ansel or Steve (since we know that Caroline doesn't play the sax). From statement 2, which is false, Steve plays the piano or the bass. From statement 4, which is false, Ansel plays the guitar, the piano, or the bass. Therefore, statement 6 is false.

Assume that statement 7 is the true statement. If so, the drums are played by Steve, Ansel, or Al. However, from statement 2, which is false, Steve plays the piano or the bass. From statement 4, which is false, Ansel's instrument is the guitar, the piano, or the bass. From statement 3, which would be false, Al plays the guitar and Ansel plays the piano. Therefore, statement 7 is false.

Therefore, statement 3 is the true statement. The guitar is played by Roger or Steve. From statement 2, Steve plays the piano or the bass. Therefore, Roger plays the guitar. From statement 4, Ansel plays the piano or the bass. From statement 3, Ansel doesn't play the piano. Therefore, he plays the bass. Therefore, Steve plays the piano. From statement 6, Al plays the sax. Therefore, Caroline plays the drums.

∾ Summary Solutions—

Ansel	bass
Caroline	drums
Al	sax
Roger	guitar
Steve	piano

PART II
FALSE LOGIC
▬▬▬

THE CASES OF
INSPECTOR DETWEILER

WHO STOLE THE STRADIVARIUS?

∾ **Considerations**—The guilty suspect's statement is false; the others are true.

Assume that A is guilty. If so, A's statement is false. If so, this means that the other three must have made true statements. However, B says C is guilty; if A is guilty, A and B have both made false statements. Therefore, A is not guilty.

Assume that C is guilty. If so, B's statement, indicating that C is guilty, is true. However, if C is guilty, C's and D's statements are both false. Therefore, C is not guilty.

Assume that D is guilty. If so, B's statement indicating that C is guilty is false. Therefore, D is not guilty.

B is guilty. The other three make true statements:

A.	T
B.	F
C.	T
D.	T

∽ **Summary Solutions**—B is the thief.

TWO PICKPOCKETS

∽ **Considerations**—The two guilty ones each make only one true statement.

Assume that B is guilty. If so, B's first statement is true, as is either the second or third statement. Therefore, B is not one of the guilty ones. Assume that C is guilty. Since C's second statement indicates that B is not guilty, it is true. Also, if C is guilty, C's third statement must also be true. Therefore C is not guilty and the two guilty ones are A and D.

	1	2	3
A	F	F	T
B	F	F	T
C	F	T	F
D	T	F	F

∽ **Summary Solutions**—A and D are the guilty ones.

THE POACHER

∽ **Considerations**—Consider that the guilty suspect makes only one true statement.

Assume that A is guilty. If so, A's first statement indicating that D is innocent is true, as is his third statement, confirming that hunting is a source of food. Therefore, A is not guilty.

Assume that B is guilty. If so, B's second statement confirming that A is not the poacher is true, as is B's third statement indicating that his statements are not all true. Therefore B is not guilty.

Assume that D is guilty. D's first statement indicates that A's statements are not all true. If the statement is false, then A's first statement that D is innocent must be true. D's second statement, that at least one of C's statements is true, must itself be true if D is the poacher as claimed by C's second statement. Either D is innocent as confirmed by A's first statement, or else D has made two true statements. Therefore, D is not guilty. Therefore, C is guilty.

	1	2	3
A	T	T	T
B	F	T	T
C	F	F	T
D	F	T	T/F

∽ **Summary Solutions**—C is the poacher.

PROPERTY DESTRUCTION AT THE VILLAGE INN

SOLUTIONS
Part II. False Logic

∾ **Considerations**—The butcher's first statement is false, as all five were present. The baker's first statement agrees with the butcher's false first statement. Therefore, it also is false.

The blacksmith's second statement is clearly false, from the description of the incident. The cobbler's first and third statements are contradictory. One is true and the other is false.

Therefore, the candlestick maker must be the one who makes no false statements. As indicated by his third statement, the baker did it.

	1	2	3	4
butcher	F	F	F	–
baker	F	T	F	–
candlestick maker	T	T	T	T
blacksmith	T	F	T	T
cobbler	F	F	T	F

∾ **Summary Solutions**—The baker is guilty.

TWO ARE GUILTY

∾ **Considerations**—Consider that one of the two culprits makes two true statements; the other makes two false statements.

Assume that A is guilty. If so, both statements are false. If so, B is also guilty. If so, B's statements must both be true. However, B's first statement claims innocence. Therefore, A is not guilty.

Assume that B is guilty. If so, since B claims innocence, both statements must be false. Therefore, if B is guilty, E's first statement must be true. However, since we know that at least A is innocent, E's first statement is false, as truthfully indicated by B. Therefore, B is not guilty.

Assume that E is guilty. If so, since we know E's first statement is false, both of his statements must be false. However, since we know that D's second statement is true, E's second statement is true. Therefore E is not guilty.

Therefore, the guilty ones are C, both of whose statements are false, and D, both of whose statements are true.

	1	**2**
A	T/F	T
B	T	T
C	F	F
D	T	T
E	F	T

∾ **Summary Solutions**—C and D are the guilty ones.

PICKPOCKET THEFTS

∾ **Considerations**—If either A or C is guilty, each of the four suspects makes two true statements. Assume that A is guilty. If so, his first statement is false, since it was given that all four suspects were in town at the time of the last known theft. A's second statement would also be false. Therefore, A is not guilty.

Assume that C is guilty. If so, A's first and third statements are false, as are C's first and second statements. Therefore, C did not do it.

The guilty suspect must be B or D. Therefore, no two of the suspects make the same number of true statements. Therefore, one makes three true statements, one makes two true statements, one makes one true statement, and one makes no true statements.

Assume that B is guilty. If so, B's second and third statements are false and first statement is true; C's first and second statements are false and third statement is true. Therefore, B did not do it. Therefore, D is guilty. C's statements are all false; A makes one true statement; D makes two true statements; and all three of B's statements are true.

	1	2	3
A	F	F	T
B	T	T	T
C	F	F	F
D	T	F	T

∾ **Summary Solutions**—D is the pickpocket.

D IS MISSING

∾ **Considerations**—Each suspect makes two true and one false statement.

A's second statement and C's second statement are contradictory. One is true and one is false. Assume that C's second statement is false. If so, C's first and third statements must be true. If so, B's second statement is false, and first and third statements are true. This means that A's third statement and second statement are true, and first statement is false. However, if A's first statement is false, this contradicts B's first statement. Therefore, C's second statement is true.

A's second statement is false, and first and third statements are true. B's second statement is false, and first and third statements are true. C's second and third statements are true, and first statement is false. C is guilty.

	1	2	3
A	T	F	T
B	T	F	T
C	F	T	T

∾ **Summary Solutions**—C is the burglar.

THE UNLUCKY CAR THIEF

∾ **Considerations**—Consider that six statements are false. A's first statement and C's first statement contradict each other. One of them is false. C's third statement and D's second statement contradict each other. One of them is false. Therefore, there are four additional false statements.

Assume A is guilty. If so, A's second statement, B's second statement, and D's first statement are the additional false statements. This makes a total of five false statements. Therefore, A is not guilty.

Assume C is guilty. If so, A's second statement and D's first and third statements are false. This makes a total of five false statements. Therefore, C is not guilty.

Assume that D is guilty. If so, A's second statement, B's first statement, and D's third statement are false. Again, this makes a total of five false statements. Therefore, D did not do it.

Therefore, B is the culprit. B's third statement, C's second statement, and D's first and third statements are the additional false statements.

	1	2	3
A	T/F	T	T
B	T	T	F
C	F/T	F	T/F
D	F	F/T	F

∾ **Summary Solutions**—B did it.

THE OLDEST OR THE YOUNGEST

〰 **Considerations**—Each suspect makes only one true statement.

B's first statement and C's first statement are contradictory. One is true and one is false. B's second statement and C's third statement are contradictory. One is true and one is false. Since each makes only one true statement, B's third statement and C's second statement are both false. D is not the youngest, and C is not the oldest.

If A's first statement is true, the conclusion from A's second statement, which would be false, would be that B, the oldest, is guilty. From A's third statement, also false, we would conclude that C was also guilty. Therefore, A's first statement is false; B is not the oldest.

If D's second statement is true, B is guilty. However, from D's first statement, which would be false, we would conclude that the oldest was guilty. Since we know that B is not the oldest (A's false first statement), D's second statement is false. D's third statement is false, since it agrees with B's third statement, which we know to be false. Therefore D's first statement is true; the guilty one is the youngest.

Conclusions at this point are: A's second statement agrees with D's first statement. Therefore, it is true, and A's third statement, that C is innocent, is false; C did it.

SOLUTIONS
Part II. False Logic

	1	2	3	oldest	youngest
A	F				
B			F	–	
C		F		–	
D	T	F	F		–

〰 **Summary Solutions**—C, the youngest, is guilty.

THE DRAGONS OF LIDD
TWO DRAGONS

∿ **Considerations**—From A's first statement, he must be a rational. If A were a predator, he would lie and say he was red. He could be a gray rational that has spoken truthfully or a red rational that has lied. Since A's second statement is true, he is a gray rational.

B's first statement is a lie, as we know that A is a rational. Therefore, B's second statement is also a lie. B is a gray predator.

∿ **Summary Solutions**—

A. gray rational

B. gray predator

TWO MORE DRAGONS

∿ **Considerations**—From B's second statement we can determine his type, whether or not he is telling the truth. Both gray and red rationals would claim to be gray; a gray predator would claim to be red, and a red predator would speak the truth. There, B is a gray or red predator.

From A's first statement we can conclude that his statements are false, and from his second statement we can conclude that B's statements are true. A is a gray predator. B is a red predator.

∿ Summary Solutions—

A. gray predator

B. red predator

THREE TO ONE

∿ **Considerations**—Assume that C's second statement, that A is red, is true. If so, from A's first statement, that he is not a predator, he must be a red rational. However, red rationals always lie and red predators always speak the truth. Therefore, C's second statement is false. A is either a gray predator or a gray rational.

From C's first statement, which we know to be false, all three are not rationals. From C's third statement, which is also false, we can conclude that B is gray. This is consistent with A's second statement. Therefore, A has spoken the truth. A is a gray rational.

B's third statement, that A's statements are true, is true. Therefore, B is a gray rational. From C's first statement, which is false, C must be a gray predator.

∿ Summary Solutions—

A. gray rational

B. gray rational

C. gray predator

THREE TO ONE AGAIN

∾ **Considerations**—If either part of a statement is false, the statement is false. Therefore, since rationals do not eat people, A has spoken falsely: he is either a red rational or a gray predator. A's second statement must be false. Therefore, either one or both of B and C are rationals.

C's third statement, that claims that A's second statement is false, is true. Therefore, he is a gray ra-tional, as indicated by his second statement. From C's first statement, A and B are both predators.

From B's statements, which are false, A and B are both gray.

∾ **Summary Solutions**—

   A. gray predator

   B. gray predator

   C. gray rational

WHOSE COLORS ARE THE SAME?

∾ **Considerations**—B's second statement is that he is not red. If the statement is true, B must be a gray rational; if it is false, he must be a red rational. Therefore, it is evident that dragon C's first statement is false, as is his second statement: dragon C and dragon A are not the same color.

Therefore, dragon A's second statement is true, as is his first statement. Dragon A is a gray rational; dragon C must be a red rational; and dragon B, whose statements are true, is a gray rational.

∾ **Summary Solutions—**

A. gray rational

B. gray rational

C. red rational

THREE ON THREE

∾ **Considerations—**Assume that A's second statement is true. If so, he's a gray rational and B and C are predators. B's second statement would be true, so he would be a red predator. Therefore, from B's first statement, C would be a red predator, too. But then C's second statement would be false, which is impossible. So A's second statement is false; he is not a rational, and, since he lied, he's a gray predator. B's first statement is false, so his second statement is also false. He, too, is a gray predator. Since A's first statement is false, C must be a rational. Since his statements are both true, he's gray.

∾ **Summary Solutions—**

A. gray predator

B. gray predator

C. gray rational

ARE THERE ANY PREDATORS LEFT?

∾ **Considerations**—Assume that A's statements are true. If so, B's second statement and A's second statements are true, and C is a red predator. However, if so, C has spoken the truth. From C's first statement, both A and B are predators, which means that B's first statement is false. Therefore, A's statements are false, and from A's first statement, B's statements are also false.

From A's second statement, which is false, C is gray, and from B's second statement, which is false, C is a rational. Therefore, from C's statements, A and B are both gray predators.

∾ **Summary Solutions**—

   A. gray predator

   B. gray predator

   C. gray rational

HOW MANY ARE RATIONALS?

∾ **Considerations**—Between B and C, it is clear that one speaks the truth and one lies. Assume that C speaks the truth. If so, since B's third statement is false, A's third statement must be true. If so, from A's first statement, A is a red predator. However, this contradicts C's second statement. Therefore, B speaks the truth and C lies. B is a gray rational. From B's third statement, A lies. From C's first statement, which we know to be false, A would falsely claim to be a predator. Therefore, A is a red rational; and from A's second statement, which we know to be false, C would falsely claim to be gray. Therefore, C is also a red rational.

∾ Summary Solutions—

A. red rational

B. gray rational

C. red rational

THREE ON THREE AGAIN

∾ **Considerations**—Between A and B, it is apparent from their first statements that one is speaking the truth and one is lying.

Assume that B's statements are true. If so, from B's second statement, C would confirm B's statement. However, C's second statement supports A's first statement. Therefore, B's statements are false. A's statements are true, as are C's statements, as confirmed by A's second statement. A is a red predator, as indicated by C.

From C's first statement, B, whose statements are false, is a gray predator, and C is a gray rational.

∾ Summary Solutions—

A. red predator

B. gray predator

C. gray rational

THE DRAGONS FROM WONK

ONE IS BLUE

∾ **Considerations**—B has given himself away. Only a blue dragon from Wonk could make his first statement. A dragon from the Kingdom of Lidd would have to deny being a red rational or a gray predator. Therefore, from B's second statement, A is a rational, as he claims. Since he has spoken the truth, A is a gray rational and B is a blue predator.

∾ **Summary Solutions**—
   A. gray rational
   B. blue predator

TWO OF THREE ARE BLUE

∾ **Considerations**—From B's first statement, we can conclude that B is either a gray predator or a red predator. If he were a blue dragon, his statement would be true. Therefore, A and C are the two blue dragons.

From A's statement, that he is a rational, we can conclude that he is a predator. From C's statement, he is a rational.

B's second statement is true. Therefore, B is a red predator.

∾ **Summary Solutions**—
   A. blue predator
   B. red predator
   C. blue rational

ONE OF THREE IS BLUE

∾ **Considerations**—From C's second statement we can conclude that he is not the blue dragon. He is either a red rational or a gray predator.

From C's first statement, which is false, A's first statement is true, B is the blue dragon. From A's second statement, B and C are predators and C is gray. A is a gray rational.

∾ **Summary Solutions**—

   A. gray rational

   B. blue predator

   C. gray predator

AT LEAST ONE IS A BLUE DRAGON

∾ **Considerations**—From B's second statement, we can conclude that B is not a blue dragon. He is either a red rational or a gray predator. D, whose first statement confirms that B is not blue, has made a true statement. He is either a gray rational or a red predator. Either A or C or both are blue.

B's first statement, that C is a predator, is false. Therefore, C is a rational. C's first statement, that he is a predator, is false. Therefore, C's second statement, that A is not a blue dragon, is false; A is a blue dragon. From A's third statement, that only one is a blue dragon, we can conclude that C is a second blue dragon. D's second statement, that B would state that A is a predator, indicates that A is a rational.

A's second statement, that C would state that D is a predator, is false. C would falsely state that D is a rational. D is a red predator. C's third statement, that three are rationals, is false. Therefore, B must be a gray predator.

∾ Summary Solutions—

A. blue rational

B. gray predator

C. blue rational

D. red predator

HOW MANY BLUE DRAGONS?

∿ **Considerations**—Assume that A's first statement is true. If so, C's first statement and B's first statements are both true. If so, D's second statement, that A is a rational, must be true, as it is consistent with B's first statement. However, A's second statement, that D is blue, conflicts with our assumption. Therefore, A's statements are false, as are B's and C's statements.

From C's third statement, we can conclude that D's statements are true. From D's second statement, A is a rational, and from D's first statement, B, C, and D are predators.

Since his statements are true, D is a red predator. From D's second statement A is a red rational. From B's and C's second statements, which are false, we can conclude that two, B and C, are blue dragons.

∿ **Summary Solutions**—

   A. red rational

   B. blue predator

   C. blue predator

   D. red predator

HYPERBOREA

WHICH ROAD TO TAKE

∿ **Considerations**—One is a Sororean and one is a Nororean.

Assume that A is the Sororean, who always speaks truthfully. If so, he truthfully answered Apollo's first inquiry and the road to the left is the one to take. However, Apollo also asked A how B would respond. If so, A would truthfully say that B, who would respond falsely, would say to take the road to the right.

Therefore, A must be the Nororean, who has answered falsely to both questions. B is the Sororean. Apollo should take the road to the right.

∿ **Summary Solutions**—

A. Nororean

B. Sororean

Apollo should take the road to the right.

APOLLO GOES DOWN THE ROAD

∿ **Considerations**—A cannot be a Sororean, as his first statement would be false, and Sororeans always speak truthfully. A cannot be a Nororean, as his first statement would be truthful, and Nororeans always speak falsely. Therefore, A is a Midrorean. His first statement is false and second statement is true: neither is a Sororean. B's statements are both false. Therefore, B is a Nororean.

∾ **Summary Solutions—**

A. Midrorean

B. Nororean

SOME JUST LIKE TO BE DIFFICULT

∾ **Considerations**—A's first statement is true. If he were a Sororean, he would truthfully say so. The statement could not be made by a Nororean. Therefore, A is a Midrorean, and his second statement is false. C is not a Midrorean.

Therefore, C's first statement is true. C is a Sororean. From C's second statement, B is a Nororean.

∾ **Summary Solutions—**

A. Midrorean

B. Nororean

C. Sororean

ONE SPEAKS TRUTHFULLY

∾ **Considerations**—One speaker is a Sororean, one is a Nororean, and one is a Midrorean.

Assume that A is the Sororean. If so, A's first statement is true: C is the Nororean. If so, B must be the Midrorean. However, C's first statement is that B is the Midrorean. This would be true—not possible for a Nororean. Therefore, A is not the Sororean.

Assume that C is the Sororean. If so, C's first statement that B is the Midrorean would be true. If so, B's first statement would be false and his second statement, that A is the Nororean, would be true. How-ever, A's second statement, that B is not the Sororean, would be true. Again, this is not possible for a Nororean. Therefore, C is not the Sororean.

Therefore, B is the Sororean. As indicated by B's second statement, A is the Nororean. C is the Midrorean, whose first statement is false and second statement is true.

∾ Summary Solutions—

A. Nororean

B. Sororean

C. Midrorean

APOLLO MAKES ONE LAST TRY

∾ **Considerations**—One is Sororean, one Nororean, and one Midrorean.

Assume that A is the Sororean. If so, from A's second statement, B would be the Nororean. Therefore, C would be the Midrorean. But A's first statement contradicts this. Therefore, A is not the Sororean.

Assume that B is the Sororean. If so, from B's second statement, C is the Midrorean. This makes A the Nororean. However, from A's third statement, which would be true, A could not be the Nororean. Therefore, C must be the Sororean. B is the Nororean, and A is the Midrorean. A's first and third statements are false and second statement is true.

∾ **Summary Solutions—**

A. Midrorean

B. Nororean

C. Sororean

SUNFLOWERS GALORE

∾ **Considerations—**The group or groups to which the four speakers belong are unknown.

A's and B's first statements are both true. B's second statement is false, as we know there are only three groups, and there are four speakers. Therefore, B is a Midrorean.

A's second statement must be false. If it were true, it would be a contradiction, as A would be a Sororean and we know B to be a Midrorean. Therefore, A is a Midrorean.

C's first statement is false, as the valuableness of sunflowers to the inhabitants is a given. C's second statement, which agrees with A's false second statement, is also false. Therefore, C is a Nororean.

D's first statement, agreeing with B's second statement, which is false, is also false. D's second statement is also false. D is a Nororean.

∾ **Summary Solutions—**

A. Midrorean

B. Midrorean

C. Nororean

D. Nororean

WHO'S AN OUTLIER?

∿ **Considerations**—Consider that one is a Sororean; one is a Nororean; one is a Midrorean; and one is an Outlier.

If B's second statement is true, A is the Sororean, and, as A's first statement indicates, B is the Outlier. If so, B's first statement, denying that he is the Outlier, is false. If so, his third statement is true. However, his third statement disputes A's second statement. Therefore, A is not the Sororean.

Since B claims that A is the Sororean, B is not the Sororean.

C, who claims to be the Outlier, is not the Sororean.

Therefore, D is the Sororean.

From D's first statement, which is true, B is not the Outlier. From D's second statement, A's third statement is true.

Therefore, A, whose first statement is false and third statement is true, is the Outlier.

B, whose first statement is true and second statement is false, is the Midrorean. B's third statement is true.

A's second statement is false.

Therefore, C is the Nororean, whose statements are all false.

∿ **Summary Solutions**—

   A. Outlier

   B. Midrorean

   C. Nororean

   D. Sororean

APOLLO MEETS AN OUTLIER

∾ **Considerations**—One and only one is an Outlier and one and only one is a Sororean. As to the other two, little is known.

A's first statement is false; there's only one Outlier. Consider A's second statement. If it is true, B is the Sororean. However, from B's third statement, if true, D is a Sororean, and, therefore, B must not be a Soro-rean. If B's first statement is false, again, B is not a Sororean. Therefore, A's second statement is false. At this point we can say that A is either a Nororean or the Outlier, and B is not the Sororean.

B's second statement, which confirms A's false first statement, is false. If B's first statement is false, B is a Nororean; if true, B must be the Outlier. Therefore, either A and B are both Nororeans or one is a Nororean and the other is the Outlier.

Assume that A is the Outlier. If so, A's fourth statement, which confirms B's third statement indicating that C is the Outlier, must be false. As to A's third statement, it is disputed by D's fourth statement, which could be true or false.

C's third statement is true, as it disputes B's second statement, which is false. C's second statement, claiming to be the Outlier, must be false. This must be the case, as, if C is the Outlier, B's fourth statement, that A is not the Outlier, is true, making B an Outlier.

Since we know there is only one Outlier, C is not an Outlier. Therefore, C must be a Midrorean.

C's first and third statements are true, and second and fourth statements are false. Therefore, D is a Sororean. D's fourth statement, disputing A's third statement, is true. A is a Nororean. B, whose first and fourth statements are true, and second and third statements are false, is the Outlier.

∾ Summary Solutions—

A. Nororean

B. Outlier

C. Midrorean

D. Sororean

PART III
WORKING WITH HYPOTHESIS

THE VOYAGES OF
SINGOOD THE SAILOR

A GIANT FISH

∾ **Considerations**—From statement 1, if the fish had just consumed a ship and several whales, it was evening. From statement 3, if it was evening, the giant fish was too old and slow. Therefore, statement 1 is not valid: the giant fish had not just consumed a ship and several whales.

From statement 4, if the giant fish was too old, it was morning. From statement 2, if it was morning, the ship and crew were too small to be noticed. Therefore, statement 4 is not valid: the giant fish was not too old and slow.

Therefore, the solution must be that it was morning and the ship and crew were too small to be noticed by the giant fish.

∾ **Summary Solutions—**

It was morning and the ship and crew were too small to be noticed by the giant fish.

AN ENCHANTED ISLAND

∾ **Considerations—**From statement 3, if A was the first mate, B was the second mate. However, from statement 2, if B was not Singood, C was the first mate. Therefore, we can conclude that A was not the first mate and, from statement 2, B was not the first mate. Therefore, C was the first mate.

From statement 1, since B was not the first mate, A was not Singood. Therefore, A was the second mate and B was Singood. (Note: Even though the assumption in statement 2 is invalid [B was Singood], this does not preclude C's being the first mate.)

∾ **Summary Solutions—**

A was the second mate

B was Singood

C was the first mate

A THIRD ISLAND

∿ **Considerations**—From statement 1, if the palms vanished first, the fruit trees were third. However, from statement 2, if the fruit trees were third to vanish, the waterfall was first. Therefore, the palms did not vanish first.

From statement 3, if the waterfall vanished first, the clear lake vanished fourth. However, from statement 4, if the clear lake was fourth, the fruit trees were first. Therefore, the waterfall was not first.

From statement 5, since neither the waterfall nor the wavy palms vanished first, the clear lake vanished first.

From statement 6, since the clear lake vanished first, the fruit trees and waterfall must have vanished second and third in some order, and the wavy palms vanished fourth.

From statement 7, since the wavy palms vanished fourth, the waterfall vanished third and the fruit trees vanished second.

∿ **Summary Solutions**—

clear lake	1st
fruit trees	2nd
waterfall	3rd
wavy palms	4th

RETURN TO THE SHIP

∾ **Considerations**—From statement 1, we can conclude that Singood was either first or third to take a turn rowing.

From statement 2, if the first mate was first to take a turn rowing, the second mate was second to take a turn. However, from statement 3, if the second mate was second to take a turn, the first mate was third in the rotation. Therefore, the assumption in statement 2, that the first mate was first to take a turn, is not valid. The first mate was either second or third in the rotation.

From statement 4, for the first mate to be third to take a turn, Singood must be second to take a turn. However, from statement 1, we know that Singood was either first or third to take a turn. Therefore, the first mate was not third. Therefore, he was second to take a turn.

From statement 5, since the second mate was not second to take a turn, the assumption that he was not third is invalid. The second mate was third and Singood was first in the rotation.

∾ **Summary Solutions**—

Singood	1st
first mate	2nd
second mate	3rd

A GIGANTIC BIRD

∿ **Considerations**—From statements 3 and 2, statement 3 is invalid: the gigantic bird's wingspan was not 40 or 50 meters wide.

From statement 4, the gigantic bird's wingspan was 20 or 30 meters wide.

Therefore, from statement 1, it carried the three shipmates 50 leagues.

∿ **Summary Solutions**—

Bird's wingspan was 20 or 30 meters wide;

it carried shipmates 50 leagues.

ATTACKED BY A GIANT SERPENT

∾ **Considerations**—From statement 1, if Singood was attacked by the serpent, the first mate stayed in the tree. If so, the second mate must have hurried to the rescue. From statement 2, if the first mate stayed in the tree, the second mate did not go to the rescue. Therefore, Singood was not attacked by the serpent.

From statement 3, if the second mate did not stay in the tree, the first mate was attacked by the serpent. Therefore, the second mate was not attacked by the serpent. Therefore, the first mate was attacked by the serpent.

From statement 4, if Singood stayed in the tree, the first mate went to the rescue. Therefore, Singood did not stay in the tree. Therefore, Singood went to the rescue, and the second mate stayed in the tree.

∾ **Summary Solutions**—

Singood	went to rescue
first mate	attacked by serpent
second mate	stayed in tree

CAPTURED BY THE ONE-EYED GIANT

∽ **Considerations**—If statement 1 is valid, then Singood's idea was to stab the giant in his one eye, the second mate's idea was to climb over the sleeping giant, and the first mate's idea was to hide under the bones. From statement 2, if the first mate's idea was to stab the giant in the eye or hide under the bones, then Singood's idea was to climb over the giant. Therefore, we can conclude that statement 1 is not valid: Singood's idea was not to stab the giant in the eye.

From statement 3, if Singood's idea was either of the other two options, then the first mate's idea was to stab the giant in the eye. Therefore, the first mate's idea was to stab the giant. From statement 2, Singood's idea was to climb over the sleeping giant, and the second mate's idea was to hide under the pile of bones.

∽ **Summary Solutions**—

Singood	climb over sleeping giant
first mate	stab giant in eye
second mate	hide under bones

SOLUTIONS
Part III. Hypotheses

ESCAPE FROM THE GIANT

〜 **Considerations**—From statement 2, if the journey took three months the escape was by climbing over the sleeping giant. From statement 3, the journey took two months if the escape was by climbing over the sleeping giant. Therefore, the journey did not take three months. Therefore, it took two months.

Statement 3 is invalid, since the escape by climbing over the sleeping giant depended on the journey's taking two months. However, from statement 1, if the journey took two months, then the escape was by hiding beneath a pile of bones.

Statement 4 is valid; the escape was not by stabbing the giant in the eye, since the journey took two months.

Therefore, the escape was by hiding beneath a pile of bones until the giant left the cave, and the journey took two months.

〜 **Summary Solutions**—

Escape made by hiding under bones; journey took two months.

AN ATTACK BY GIANT SPIDERS

∿ **Considerations**—From statement 1, since either the spider with six useful legs or the spider with seven useful legs was injured by Singood, the spider with five legs was not injured by Singood.

From statement 2, since the spider with five useful legs was not injured by Singood, the spider with seven useful legs was not injured by the second mate.

From statement 3, since the spider with five useful legs was not injured by Singood, the spider with six useful legs was not injured by the first mate. There-fore, by statement 4, the spider with seven useful legs was injured by Singood.

Therefore, it's the spider with six useful legs that was injured by the second mate, and the spider with five useful legs was injured by the first mate.

∿ **Summary Solutions**—

Singood	spider with 7 useful legs
first mate	spider with 5 useful legs
second mate	spider with 6 useful legs

SERPENTMARES!

~ **Considerations**—From statement 3, if Singood was not devoured by either the black or blue serpent, the second mate was devoured by the red serpent. Therefore, Singood was not devoured by the red serpent.

From statement 1, if the second mate was not devoured by either the blue serpent or the green serpent, the first mate was devoured by the red serpent. Therefore, the second mate was not devoured by the red serpent. Therefore, the first mate was devoured by the red serpent.

Therefore, from statement 4, Singood was not devoured by the blue serpent. Therefore, since, from statement 3, the second mate was not devoured by the red serpent, Singood was devoured by the black serpent.

From statement 2, the second mate was devoured by the green serpent. The blue serpent went away hungry.

~ **Summary Solutions**—

Singood	black serpent
first mate	red serpent
second mate	green serpent

CONTEST ON THE BEACH

∿ **Considerations**—From statement 1, if the first mate won the race down the beach, Singood won the coconut throw. If so, the second mate won the tree climb. However, from statement 3, if the second mate won the tree climb, the first mate won the coconut throw. Therefore, the first mate did not win the race down the beach.

From statement 5, if Singood won the race down the beach, the first mate won the tree climb. If so, the second mate won the coconut throw. However, from statement 2, if the second mate won the coconut throw, the first mate won the race down the beach. Therefore, Singood did not win the race down the beach. Therefore, the race was won by the second mate.

Therefore, from statement 4, Singood won the tree climb, and the first mate won the coconut throw.

∿ **Summary Solutions**—

Singood	tree climb
first mate	coconut throw
second mate	race down the beach

THE RESCUE

∼ **Considerations**—From statement 1, if the rescue ship did not have four masts, then it was the white ship. From statement 5, if the rescue ship had three masts, it was not the white ship. Therefore, it was not the white ship.

From statement 2, if the black ship was the rescue ship, it had four masts. However, from statement 3, if the rescue ship had four masts, it was not black. Therefore, it was not black.

Therefore, from statement 4, the rescue ship was green and had four masts.

∼ **Summary Solutions**—

The ship was green and had four masts.

SIR HECTOR HEROIC
THE DRAGON FIGHTER

A CONTEST

∿ **Considerations**—From statements 1 and 5, Sir Able did not win the contest. From statements 2, 6, and 4, Sir Hector did not win. Since we know that both Sir Hector and Sir Gallant camped out overnight in the backcountry, then, from statement 3, Sir Gallant was not the winner.

By elimination, Sir Bold was the contest winner.

∿ **Summary Solutions**—

Sir Bold was the contest winner.

SEEKING ADVENTURE

∿ **Considerations**—From statement 3, Sir Bold either confronted a sorcerer or battled a giant. From statement 2, either Sir Hector or Sir Able battled a giant. Therefore, Sir Bold did not battle a giant; he confronted a sorcerer.

From statement 1, if Sir Gallant did not confront a sorcerer, Sir Hector battled a dragon. Therefore, Sir Hector battled a dragon. Therefore, Sir Able battled a giant, and Sir Gallant battled a dragon.

∾ Summary Solutions—

Sir Able battled a giant.

Sir Bold confronted a sorcerer.

Sir Gallant battled a dragon.

Sir Hector battled a dragon.

THE SWORD-FIGHTING MATCHES

∾ **Considerations**—From statement 1, if Sir Hector lost, sir Able won. If so, Sir Bold also won. However, from statement 3, if Sir Bold won, Sir Hector must have also won. Therefore, Sir Hector did not lose. Therefore, from statement 2, since Sir Hector won his match, Sir Bold was the knight who lost.

∾ Summary Solutions—

Sir Bold was the knight who lost.

MURDER IN THE BLACK CASTLE

〜 **Considerations**—From statement 1, if the knight in room 1 was the culprit, the knight in room 3 was the victim. However, from statement 3, if the knight in room 3 was the victim, the knight in room 2 was the culprit. Therefore, the knight in room 1 was not the culprit. From statement 7, if the knight in room 2 was the culprit, the servant was the victim. However, from statement 5, it is clear that the servant was not the victim. Therefore, the knight in room 2 was not the culprit.

From statement 6, if the knight in room 3 was the culprit, the knight in room 2 was the victim. However, from statement 2, if the knight in room 2 was the victim, the servant was the culprit. Therefore, the knight in room 3 was not the culprit. From statement 4, if the servant was the culprit, the knight in room 3 was the victim. However, from statement 3, we know that if the knight in room 3 was the victim, the knight in room 2 was the culprit. Therefore, the servant was not the culprit. Therefore, the remaining suspect, the master, must be the culprit, and the knight in room 1, the only knight not accounted for, was the victim.

〜 **Summary Solutions**—

The master was the culprit; the knight in room 1 was the victim.

THE MYSTERIOUS MASKED MISCREANT

∾ **Considerations**—From statement 1, if Sir Hector was overwhelmed by the miscreant's evil face, it was morning. However, from statement 3, if it was morning, Sir Hector had forgotten his sword. Therefore, Sir Hector was not overwhelmed by the evil face. From statement 2, if Sir Hector's fellow knights saved him, it was early afternoon, which is inconsistent with statement 4. Therefore, the confrontation did not take place in the early afternoon, and Sir Hector's fellow knights did not arrive to save him. From statement 4, if it was early evening, then Sir Hector's fellow knights arrived just in time to save him. But this is inconsistent with statement 2. So it was not early evening. Therefore, from statement 3, it was morning and Sir Hector had forgotten his sword, so did not stay to do battle.

∾ **Summary Solutions**—

It was morning; Sir Hector had forgotten his sword, so did not stay to do battle.

WHO SAW WHICH GIANT?

∾ **Considerations**—From statement 2, if the assumption that Sir Able was not accurate in what he observed was valid, giant number two is guilty. From statement 1, if giant number one were guilty, Sir Hector was accurate in what he observed. From statement 4, if Sir Hector's description was accurate, so was Sir Bold's. However, from statement 3, it would validate the assumption in statement 2. In either case, giant number two is guilty. (Note: If Sir Hector's description were accurate, this would not necessarily preclude the assumption in statement 1 from being invalid.)

∽ Summary Solutions—

Giant number two is guilty.

SIR HECTOR'S MOST CHALLENGING ADVENTURE

∽ **Considerations**—From statement 1, neither Grimsby nor the miscreant was the most challenging unless the dragon was not the second most challenging.

From statement 2, if the confrontation with the dragon was the second most challenging, neither the rescue from the black tower nor the sorcerer was the most challenging. Therefore, the confrontation with the dragon was not the second most challenging (as this would eliminate all five adventures as most challenging), and (from statement 1) either the encounter with Grimsby or the confrontation with the masked miscreant was the most challenging. The rescue from the black tower cannot be the most challenging. Therefore, from statement 4, the confrontation with the sorcerer cannot be the second most challenging.

From statement 3, if Grimsby the Giant was not the second most challenging, the masked miscreant was the most challenging. Therefore, the masked miscreant was the most challenging.

∾ **Summary Solutions—**

The masked miscreant was the most challenging.

FOUR FAIR DAMSELS IN DISTRESS

∾ **Considerations—**From statement 4, either Maid Matilda was rescued from the miscreant's hideout, or neither she nor Maid Morgana was. From statement 1, since Maid Morgana was not rescued from the miscreant's hideout, Maid Marie was rescued from a castle tower.

From statement 3, since Maid Marie was rescued from a castle tower, Maid Mary was rescued from two giants. Therefore, from statement 2, Maid Matilda was rescued from the miscreant's hideout. Therefore, Maid Morgana must have been rescued from a dragon's lair.

∾ **Summary Solutions—**

Maid Marie	castle tower
Maid Mary	two giants
Maid Morgana	dragon's lair
Maid Matilda	miscreant's hideout

ENCOUNTER WITH A GIGANTIC SERPENTLIKE CREATURE

∾ **Considerations**—From statement 1, if Sir Gallant did the fighting, Sir Hector observed. If so, Sir Resolute went home. However, from statement 5, if Sir Hector observed, Sir Resolute did the fighting. Therefore, Sir Gallant did not do the fighting.

From statement 2, if Sir Hector did the fighting, Sir Gallant went home. If so, Sir Resolute observed. However, from statement 4, if Sir Resolute observed, Sir Gallant did the fighting. Therefore, Sir Hector did not do the fighting. Therefore, Sir Resolute must have done the fighting.

From statement 3, if Sir Gallant went home, Sir Resolute observed. However, since we know that Sir Resolute did the fighting, Sir Gallant did not go home. Therefore, Sir Gallant observed, and Sir Hector went home.

∾ **Summary Solutions**—

Sir Resolute	did fighting
Sir Gallant	observed
Sir Hector	went home

CONFRONTATION WITH THE GIANT

∿ **Considerations**—Consider the assumption in statement 1 to be valid. If so, Sir Gallant was one of the two who confronted the giant. If the assumption is invalid, either Sir Hector or Sir Victor was one of the two who confronted the giant. Therefore, whether or not the assumption in statement 1 is valid or invalid, we can conclude that the pair who confronted the giant were not Sir Able and Sir Bold, Sir Able and Sir Resolute, or Sir Bold and Sir Resolute.

From statement 3, the two who confronted the giant were not Sir Bold and Sir Gallant, Sir Bold and Sir Victor, or Sir Gallant and Sir Victor.

From statement 4, the two who confronted the giant were not Sir Hector and Sir Gallant, Sir Hector and Sir Resolute, or Sir Gallant and Sir Resolute.

From statement 5, Sir Hector did not confront the giant, since we know that, from statement 4, he did not confront the giant along with either Sir Gallant or Sir Resolute.

From statement 6, Sir Victor must have been one of the two who confronted the giant, as the statement identifies three of the four knights not eliminated.

From statement 2, since Sir Victor was one of the two who confronted the giant, the other, by elimination, must have been Sir Resolute.

∿ **Summary Solutions**—

Sir Resolute and Sir Victor confronted the giant.

VICTORY AT
THE GRAND TOURNAMENT

∾ **Considerations**—From statement 1, if Sir Gallant was victorious, Sir Hector was not victorious. If so, Sir Able, Sir Bold, or Sir Resolute was also victorious. From statement 2, if Sir Able was victorious, Sir Gallant was not victorious; and from statement 4, if Sir Resolute was victorious, then Sir Able was victorious; and from statement 3, if Sir Hector was not victorious, neither was Sir Bold victorious. Therefore, Sir Gallant was not one of the two victorious knights.

From statement 5, if Sir Bold was victorious, Sir Able was not victorious. If so, Sir Gallant, Sir Hector, or Sir Resolute was also victorious. However, we know Sir Gallant was not victorious; and from statement 4, Sir Resolute's being victorious depends on Sir Able's being victorious; and from statement 6, Sir Hector's being victorious depends on Sir Resolute's being victorious. Therefore, Sir Bold was not one of the two victorious knights.

From statement 6, if Sir Hector was victorious, Sir Resolute was victorious. From statement 4, Sir Resolute's being victorious relies on Sir Able's being victorious. Therefore, Sir Hector was not victorious.

∾ **Summary Solutions**—

The two victorious knights were Sir Able and Sir Resolute.

KNIGHTS' ADVERSARIES

〜 **Considerations**—Consider statement 4: if Sir Gallant's skill was not dealing with dragons, then his skill was not dealing with giants, as the skill would belong to Sir Hector.

From statement 7, Sir Able could not be the most skilled at dealing with giants, as if Sir Gallant's skill was not dealing with dragons, then (from statement 4) Sir Hector's skill was dealing with giants.

From statement 6, as we know that Sir Able was not the most skilled at dealing with giants, Sir Hector's skill was not dealing with sorcerers. Therefore, from statement 2, Sir Bold's skill was not dealing with giants. Therefore, Sir Hector was the most skilled at dealing with giants.

From statement 1, Sir Able was not the most skilled at dealing with dragons. From statement 3, since Sir Able's skill was not dealing with dragons, Sir Bold's skill was not dealing with sorcerers.

Therefore, Sir Able's skill was dealing with sorcerers. Sir Gallant and Sir Bold dealt, in some order, with giant serpents and dragons. But from statement 5, Sir Gallant could not have dealt with giant serpents. Therefore, Sir Gallant's skill was dealing with dragons, and Sir Bold dealt with giant serpents.

〜 **Summary Solutions—**

Sir Able's skill	sorcerers
Sir Bold's skill	giant serpents
Sir Gallant's skill	dragons
Sir Hector's skill	gia

THREE NOVELS

THE CARD PLAYERS

Chapter 1: The Scorekeeper

The following reasoning uses [I] and [II].

Let **M** represent a man, **WÓ** represent one woman, **WÔ** represent the other woman, and **E** represent the empty chair. Then, from [1], the men and women were seated around the table in one of the following two ways, with the scorekeeper's symbol circled.

Let **MÓ** represent the husband of **WÓ**. Then, from [2], the two ways may be further clarified as shown below.

Then, from [2], the scorekeeper must be the husband of **WÔ**.

Then, from [3], **MÓ** cannot be the widower's son, since he is younger than the widower, so it must be the widower's daughter's husband. So *the scorekeeper was the widower's son.*

Chapter 2: The Cheater

The following reasoning uses [I] and [II].

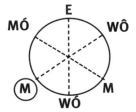
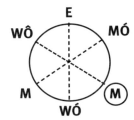

Suppose the widower's daughter's husband is the cheater and the only man who lied, from [4] and [6]. Then, from [1], the widower sat directly across from his daughter. Then, from [5] and [6], the widower's daughter's husband sat next to the widower. Then, from [2], the widower's son sat directly across from the widower's daughter's husband. Then, from [3], the widower sat next to the empty chair. Then the widower's daughter's husband sat next to the widower's son's wife. In summary, the seating arrangement would be the one shown below or one that is counterclockwise to it.

Since this arrangement has the widower's daughter's husband as the cheater, it contradicts [5]. So, the widower's daughter's husband is not the cheater and he did not lie.

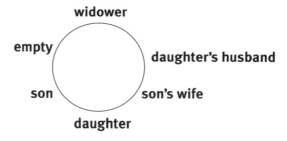

Suppose the widower's son is the cheater and the only man who lied, from [4] and [6]. Then, from [1], the widower sat directly across from his daughter. Then, from [5] and [6], the widower's son sat next to the widower. Then, from [3], the widower's son's wife sat next to the widower's son. Then, from [2], the widower's son sat directly across from the empty chair. Then the widower's daughter's husband sat next to the widower. In summary, the seating arrangement would be the one shown below or one that is counterclockwise to it.

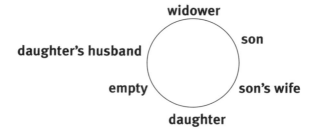

Since this arrangement has the widower's son as the cheater, it contradicts [5]. So the widower's son is not the cheater and he did not lie.

Then, from [4] and [6], the widower lied and the cheater was the widower. Then the widower's daughter's husband and the widower's son both told the truth; so, from [3], the widower's daughter's husband sat next to the empty chair and, from [2], the widower's son sat directly across from the widower's daughter's husband. Then, from [5] and [6], the widower sat next to the empty chair. Then—from [1], [4], and [6]—the widower sat directly across from the widower's son's wife. Then the widower's daughter sat directly across from the empty chair. In summary, the seating arrangement would be the one shown below or one that is counterclockwise to it.

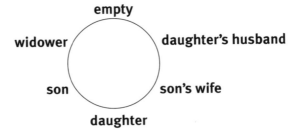

Chapter 3: The Empty Chair

The following reasoning uses [I] and [II].

Let **M** represent a man, **W** represent a woman, and **E** represent the empty chair. Then, from [5], the men and women were seated around the table in one of the following ways.

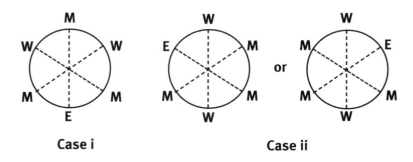

In Case i: Each woman sat directly across from a man. So, from [4], the widower's son's wife sat directly across from the widower. But, since the widower sat directly across from a woman, he sat directly across from his daughter, from [3]. This situation is impossible. So Case i is not the correct one.

Then Case ii is the correct one. From [1], if the widower's son sat directly across from a man, then the widower's son sat directly across from the widower's daughter's husband. Then the widower's daughter's husband sat directly across from the widower's son, contradicting [2]. So the widower's son did not sit directly across from a man, but the widower's son sat directly across from the empty chair. Then the widower's daughter's husband sat directly across from the widower and, from [2], next to the widower's son. Then each woman sat in either one of the two remaining positions.

Chapter 4: Death of a Card Player

The following reasoning uses [I] and [II].

Let **M** represent a man, **W** represent a woman, and **E** represent the empty chair. Then, from [2], the men and women were seated around the table in one of the following ways.

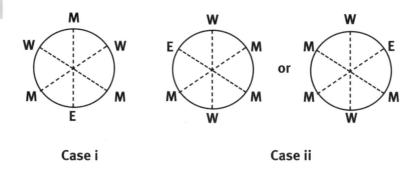

Case i   **Case ii**

In both Case i and Case ii: if the widower's son and the widower's son's wife both told the truth in [5] and [6], then the hypothesis in their statements must be false; so the widower sat directly across from the empty chair. Then the hypothesis in the widower's daughter's statement and in the widower's daughter's husband's statement, in [3] and [4], must be false; so all four suspects told the truth. This situation contradicts [1] and [7]; so either the widower's son in [5] lied or the widower's son's wife in [6] lied. Then the hypothesis in [5] and [6] is true and someone sat directly across from the widower.

If the widower's son lied in [5], then Case ii cannot be the correct case because the widower's son's wife would also have lied in [6], contradicting [1] and [7]. So Case i is the correct case. Since someone sat directly across from the widower, the widower sat directly across from a woman, namely the widower's son's wife, who told the truth in [6]. Then the widower sat next to only one person (and the empty chair), and that person must have been his daughter. So, from [3], the widower's daughter also lied. This situation is impossible because it contradicts [1] and [7].

So the widower's son's wife lied and, from [1] and [7], the murderer was the widower's son's wife. Then, since someone sat directly across from the widower and the widower's daughter's husband told the truth, Case ii is the correct case and the widower's son sat directly across from the widower. The widower may have sat between his son's wife and the empty chair, between his son's wife and his daughter's husband, or between his daughter and his daughter's husband.

A COMPANY OF ACTORS

Chapter 1: The Playwright

The following reasoning uses [I] and [II].

From [2] and [3], if Anita and Brian are each in a room shown below marked with an x, then Chloe and David are each in a room shown below marked with a y.

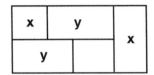 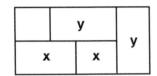

So either Chloe or David is in the large room that borders on all the other rooms, and the other is in a large room also; see below (C represents Chloe and D represents David).

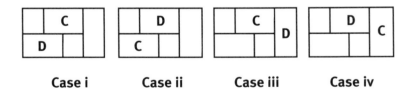

Case i   Case ii   Case iii   Case iv

Then, from [2], Ellen (represented by E) is in the room shown below.

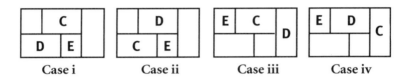

Case i   Case ii   Case iii   Case iv

From [4], Cases iii and iv are eliminated, and Cases i and ii are as shown below (A represents Anita and B represents Brian).

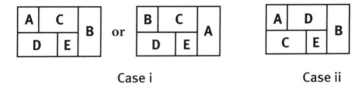

Case i   Case ii

Then, from [1], both parts of Case i are eliminated—because more than one room borders on exactly two other woman-occupied rooms (Brian's and Chloe's, all except Brian's)—and *Chloe was the playwright.*

Chapter 2: The Whistler

The following reasoning uses [I] and [II].

From [1], the dressing rooms were occupied in the following way (**A** represents Anita, etc.).

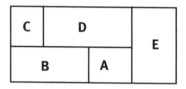

From [2] and [3] and assuming each actor in turn was the whistler, the truth or falsity of each characteristic is as follows (**t** represents true and **f** represents false).

| Actor as whistler | Characteristic | | | | |
	i	ii	iii	iv	v
Anita	f	t	f	t	t
Brian	t	f	t	t	f
Chloe	f	t	f	t	f
David	t	f	t	f	t
Edith	t	t	f	t	f

From [4], *Chloe was the whistler* because she is the only actor with other than three correct characteristics; she has only two.

Chapter 3: The Director

The following reasoning uses [I] and [II].

From [1], the dressing rooms were occupied in the following way (**A** represents Anita, etc.).

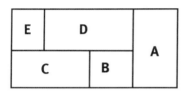

From [2], the director had a sibling. So if both hypotheses in [4] and [6] are true, then both conclusions cannot be true (they are contradictory); and if the hypothesis in [6] is true, then the hypothesis in [4] is true. So the hypothesis in [6] is not true and (a) the dressing room of the director did not border on more rooms than the dressing room of the director's sibling. Then, from [1], the director was not David.

Suppose that the director and the director's sibling had rooms that bordered on each other. Then, from [1] and [3], the possibilities for director and director's sibling are the following (**B** represents Brian, etc.).

	i	ii	iii	iv
Director	**B**	**B**	**C**	**E**
Director's sibling	**A**	**C**	**E**	**C**

Possibility (i) is eliminated, from [4] or [5]. Possibilities (ii) and (iv) are eliminated, from [5]. Possibility (iii) is eliminated, from [6]. So (b) the director and the director's sibling had dressing rooms that did not border on each other.

Then, from (a) and (b), the possibilities for director and director's sibling are the following (**A** represents Anita, etc.).

	v	vi	vii	viii	ix	x
Director	A	A	B	C	E	E
Director's sibling	C	E	E	A	A	B

Possibility (vii) is eliminated, from [4] or because the hypothesis in [6] is not true. Possibility (viii) is eliminated, from [6]. Possibility (ix) is eliminated, from [5]. Possibility (x) is eliminated, from [4]. So either Possibility (v) or (vi) is correct and *Anita was the director*. Then the director's sibling was either Chloe or Edith.

Chapter 4: Death of an Actor

The following reasoning uses [I] and [II].

From [3], since three actors lied, at least three of the hypotheses in [2] are true; so the murderer of Edith is one of the other four actors.

In [2], the hypothesis of Brian's statement contradicts the hypothesis of Chloe's statement; so one of these hypotheses is true and the other is false. If Chloe's hypothesis is the false one, then her statement is the only true one, from [3]. Then Brian's hypothesis must be true and his conclusion must be false. But if

Brian's conclusion is false, then David's conclusion must be true, so that David's statement is true. This situation contradicts [3] (both Chloe's statement and David's statement are true). So it is Brian's hypothesis that is the false one and his statement is the only true one. Then, from [3], all of Anita's, Chloe's, and David's hypotheses are true and all of their conclusions are false. Then, since David's conclusion is false, Brian's conclusion is true.

Since Anita's conclusion is false, Anita's room and David's room are the same size. Then, from [1], Anita and David both have large rooms.

Since Brian's conclusion is true, Brian's room and David's room are different sizes. So Brian has a small room, the one that is not Edith's.

Then, since Chloe's conclusion is false, Chloe's room does not border on Brian's room. So the rooms are occupied in one of the two ways shown below (A represents Anita, etc.).

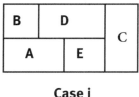
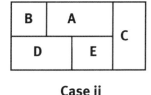

Case i   **Case ii**

SOLUTIONS
Part III. Hypotheses

Since both of Anita's and David's hypotheses are true, the murderer's room and the victim's room border on the same total number of other rooms, namely three. So, looking only at this total number of other rooms, the murderer is Anita in Case i and David in Case ii. Edith's room borders on one other man-occupied room and two other woman-occupied rooms in each case, but only in Case ii does the murderer's room border on one other man-occupied room and two other woman-occupied rooms. So Case ii is the correct one and David was the murderer.

THE GOURMET DINERS

Chapter 1: The President of the Club

The following reasoning uses [I] and [II].

From [3], two men sat directly across from each other, and a man and a woman sat directly across from each other. So two women sat directly across from each other and, from [3], (a) the two women who sat directly across from each other were April and Carla. Then, from [1], (b) April sat on Ellen's immediate left.

From [2], if Derek sat on Basil's immediate right, then Basil did not sit on a woman's immediate left, as required by [1]. So (c) Derek sat on Felix's immediate right. Then, from [3], (d) Felix sat directly across from Basil. Then, since April and Carla sat directly across from each other, (e) Derek sat directly across from Ellen.

The president of the club was neither April nor Carla, from [4] and (a); nor Ellen—from [4], (a), and (b); nor Felix, from [4] and (c); nor Derek, from [4] and e. *So the president of the club was Basil.*

Using (a) through (e), one can proceed to place the players

around the table in any of three ways as follows (**A** represents April, etc.). First, place Felix and Basil directly across from each other in each of the three possible positions, from (d). Secondly, place Derek, from (c). Thirdly, place Ellen, from (e). Fourthly, place April, from (b). Fifthly, place Carla, from (a).

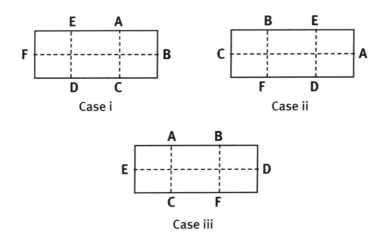

Case iii is impossible, from [2]. Cases i and ii are possible; turned upside down, each seating arrangement remains the same.

Chapter 2: The Suspected Poisoner

The following reasoning uses [I] and [II].

From [4] and [7], a woman sat on Basil's immediate left. Then, from [1] through [3], that woman lied. Then, from [4] through

[7], the diners were arranged around the table in one of the following ways—disregarding how they sat directly across from each other (B represents Basil, D represents Derek, F represents Felix, Wf represents a woman who lied, and Wt represents a woman who told the truth).

Suppose Case i is the correct way. Then, from [1] through [3], W_t is Ellen. Then, from [1] and [2], the woman on Derek's immediate left cannot have lied. This situation is impossible, so Case i is not the correct way.

Then Case ii is the correct way. Then, from [1] through [3], W_t is Ellen. Then, from [1] and [2], the woman on Derek's immediate left is April—Carla cannot have lied if she was that woman. Then the remaining woman is Carla. So, from [4] and [7], *Basil suspected Carla of trying to poison his drink.*

From Case ii, any of the three seating arrangements shown below and on the next page may be correct (A represents April, etc.). Turned upside down, each seating arrangement remains the same.

Chapter 3: The Recipe

The following reasoning uses [I] and [II].

From [1], [2], and [5], the possibilities for recipe giver and cook are the following.

	i	ii	iii	iv	v	vi
Recipe giver	Felix	Felix	Basil	Derek	Basil	Derek
Cook	Ellen	Basil	Felix	April	Ellen	Carla

From [1], [2], and [6], the possibilities for recipe giver and cook are the following.

	vii	viii	ix
Recipe giver	April	Ellen	Carla
Cook	Ellen	April	Basil

From [1], [2], and [4], Possibilities (ii) and (iii) are eliminated; and, from [3], there are no other possibilities. From the remaining possibilities, if anyone besides Derek was the recipe giver, then you would know who the cook was; but if Derek was the recipe giver, you would not know whether the cook was April or Carla. So, from [7], *Derek was the recipe giver.*

Chapter 4: Death of a Gourmet Diner

The following reasoning uses [I] and [II].

If the hypothesis in [5] is true, then the common hypothesis in [1] and [2] is true (common because directly-across-from-each-other women must occur simultaneously with directly-across-from-each-other men), or the common hypothesis in [3] and [4] is true (common because side-by-side women must occur simultaneously with side-by-side men), or both common hypotheses in [1] through [4] are true. Then, since at least four of the five conclusions in [1] through [5] are false, less than four of the five propositions are true, contradicting [6]. So the hypothesis in [5] is false. Then the men and women were seated around the table in one of the following ways (M represents a man and W represents a woman). Turned upside down, each seating arrangement remains the same.

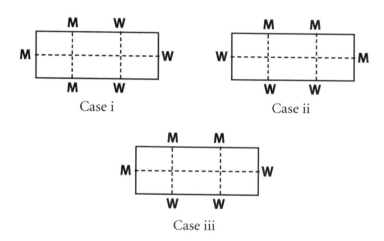

Case i

Case ii

Case iii

If Case i is a correct way, then the common hypothesis in [1] and [2] is true and the common hypothesis in [3] and [4] is true. Then, since at least three of the four conclusions in [1] through [4] are false, less than four of the five propositions are true, contradicting [6].

So Case i is not a correct way. Then only the common hypothesis in [3] and [4] is true. Then, because Ellen did not sit across from April, the conclusion in [4] is false. Then [4] is the only proposition that is false, as required by [6]. Then [3] is a true proposition; then the conclusion in [3] is true. Then *Derek was the murderer* and he sat directly across from April.

In summary:

	Hypothesis	**Conclusion**	**Proposition**
[1]	false	false	true
[2]	false	false	true
[3]	true	true	true
[4]	true	false	false
[5]	false	false	true

PART IV
COOLING DOWN

QUICK LOGIC

110. The Pacific Ocean. Even though it had not been discovered or named by Balboa, it was still the biggest ocean.

111. One cookie, because after eating one you would no longer have an empty stomach.

112. Because it wasn't raining.

113. Holes.

114. By walking and dragging the rope with it. The puzzle does not say that the leash is tied to something.

115. The number 400, to hang on a house. This number is formed by three digits, at $1 each.

116. It was daytime, so the room was light.

117. With one quarter and one nickel. The puzzle says that one of the coins is not a nickel, and it is true since a quarter is not a nickel.

118. Because he earns double by giving a haircut to two foreigners instead of to only one person in town.

119. He goes to the next room and by crawling toward the bottle, he slides into the room.

120. The plane had not yet taken off.

121. He had already put sugar in his coffee.

122. The match.

123. By serving mashed potatoes.

124. It is a male giraffe, so it is the father and not the mother of the offspring.

125. Ten cows. We can call the pigs cows, but it doesn't make them cows.

126. He must always be behind the whistle.

127. There is no reason to baptize him. If he is Catholic, he is already baptized.

128. The letter "e."

129. My uncle Emil is blind, and he was reading in Braille.

130. He is a farmer. He needs plenty of water, so if he lacks water he has no income and he won't be able to buy or even make wine.

131. At the beginning of the puzzle, it says that you are the cab driver. Therefore, the answer is your name and age.

132. One of the trains went into the tunnel hours after the other.

133. It was a girls' team.

134. My aunt Martha was a pedestrian, too.

135. The customers paid $27, $25 to cover their bill and $2 as a tip for the waiter.

136. The driver of the moped was the policeman's son.

137. The butcher's daughter is the fisherman's wife.

138. Since he's a butcher, he weighs meat.

139. The first four people pick one apple each, and the fifth one takes the basket with the apple in it.

140. Either a deep-sea diver or an astronaut.

141. "To sint" means to take off your clothes, and "to sant" is to go into the water to bathe.

142. Because before the game begins, the score is always 0-0.

143. I deposited $50 in my bank account to have enough funds to cash the check.

144. The passenger gave the driver 25 cents in the form of four nickels and five pennies.

146. As far as half of the forest, because if she went any further, she would be leaving the forest, instead of going into it.

150. The parrot was deaf.

151. The surgeon was the boy's mother.

152. Because there are fewer black sheep than white sheep.

257. Two blankets one inch thick each, because the air between them also acts as insulation.

258. No. It hasn't because the total weight of the ice is equal to the volume of water moved.

259. This can never happen. These are two contradictory concepts. If one of them exists, the other cannot possibly exist as well.

260. At the North or South Pole.

261. I must pour it before going upstairs, because the coffee will lose more heat before adding the milk rather than after. (Matter loses heat proportionally to the difference in temperature with the surrounding environment.)

LOGIC

153. She dropped her earring into her coffee beans.

154. The dictionary. The word "foreword" comes before "epilogue," "end" is in the first half of the dictionary, and "index" comes before "introduction."

155. The girl's name is Anne COUPLE.

156. If it were an authentic coin, it could not have "B.C." (This system was created after Jesus died, not before he was born.)

157. Neither country, because they are survivors.

158. What the director actually needed was a real night shift guard that did not sleep at work, even if he could predict the future in his dreams.

159. My cousin Edward is bald. Therefore, his hair cannot get wet.

160. My aunt is really short and the button for the 25th floor is at the highest point she can reach.

161. The neighbor was snoring. That is why he couldn't sleep. When he made the call, the person woke up and stopped making noise.

162. He must turn on both faucets at the same time.

163. The woman died before the operation.

164. If three of the letters are correct, the fourth one must be too. Therefore, there is only one way.

165. The same month you are reading this.

166. The river was frozen.

167. When he sees his coworker, the miner with the clean face assumes that his face is also dirty and wipes it. The miner with a dirty face sees his coworker with a clean face and assumes that his is also clean.

168. The letter "g."

169. Hairdressers don't cut their own hair. Therefore, the clean hairdresser gave the bad haircut and the dirty hairdresser gave the perfect haircut. Thus, it is better to go to the dirty salon.

170. The customer was in his firefighter uniform.

171. Because in 96 hours it would again be night.

172. It was a drive-in theater. He killed her in the car. On his way out, nobody noticed that the woman was dead in the car.

173. First he immersed the crown in a container of water and measured the level of the water. Then he removed the crown and immersed the gold bar, measuring the water level. If the levels were not the same, the gold had been mixed with another metal.

174. Two apples.

175. It will still be 38°.

176. On his birthday.

177. He took the same time in both cases, because 1 hour and 20 minutes equals 80 minutes.

178. If the cab driver had been deaf, he would not have heard the address the passenger had given to him. He only mentioned he was deaf when the passenger didn't stop talking.

182. I killed three flies. They remain. The rest would have flown away immediately.

180. If he became a widower when he was 55 and died when he was 80, he was a widower for 25 years.

181. One was standing at the main door of a bank and his friend was standing at the back door. There was 84 million dollars in the safe of the bank. Therefore, "between both of them" they had that amount of money.

262. The flotation line will be lower, because the raft will be lighter. The water level of the pool will also be lower, because the volume of water that the rocks move when they are in the raft is larger than the volume of water the rocks move when they are at the bottom of the pool. When the rocks are on the raft, they move a volume of water equal to the weight of the rocks. When the rocks are at the bottom of the pool, the volume of the water moved is equal to the actual volume of the rocks. Since rocks are denser than water, this is the smaller of the two volumes.

264. Eight times, as shown below.

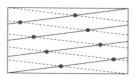

265. While the raft is loaded with the salt, he must mark the flotation line. Then, he must unload the salt and load the raft with gold until the water level reaches the flotation line. This means that the weight of the salt and the gold will be equal.

TIME

69. After being inverted twice, the hourglass continued working in its initial position. Therefore, the extra hour that it measured was a consequence of these two inversions, half an hour each time. If it was inverted for the second time at 11:30, the first time had to be a half-hour earlier, at 11:00.

70. The clock that doesn't work will show the precise time twice a day, but the fast one will take $2 \times 60 \times 12 = 1440$ days to show the precise time. Therefore, the broken clock shows the correct time more often.

72. Ten times (you can verify it yourself).

73. Four seconds (it takes two seconds between 2 consecutive strikes).

74. Four hours, the time between 8 and 12.

75. There is 1 second between 2 strikes. Therefore, it will take 11 seconds for the clock to strike 12 times.

38. 29 days. One spider would have covered half of the space on the 29th day, and on the 30th day would repeat what had been done, covering the space completely. Two spiders would each have covered half of the space in 29 days, therefore covering the entire area.

77. He would have drunk the same number of cups of coffee. The difference is that the conversation would have taken place on March 14.

78. Friday.

79. Three days and two nights. She left yesterday and will return tomorrow.

80. The man's birthday is December 31 and he was talking on January 1. He's 36 now, the day before yesterday he was 35, this calendar year he will turn 37, and next calendar year he will turn 38.

81. It happened to Gioacchino Rossini, who was born on February 29, 1792, and who died on November 13, 1868. Remember that 1800 was not a leap year. All years that are divisible by four are leap years, except those that end in "00." They are only leap years if they are divisible by 400.

WORDS

83. Neither. The yolk of an egg is yellow.

84. It is not "I am going in" or "I am not going in." The opposite is "I am leaving."

85. The word "incorrectly."

86. Lounger.

87. It's a matter of language. Consider "four twenty" as $4.20. Then it is true.

88. Yes. "Paris" starts with a "p," and "ends" starts with an "e."

89. The phone operator was trying to get the spelling of the man's last name. Therefore it makes no sense to ask, "I as in what?" The operator had already understood it was an "I."

90. The letter "i."

91. Let's suppose it is false. By saying "This statement is false," it becomes true and vice versa. Therefore, to be false it has to be true and vice versa. It is a paradox.

92. The letter "u."

93. He will not change his mind.

94. His statement must be "I will be hanged." If they want to hang him, the sentence is true, and therefore, they will not be able to hang him. For the same reason, he cannot be drowned because his statement would be false and they could not drown him if his statement is false. (Based on Don Quixote, by Cervantes.)

FAMILY TIES

95. Yes, as long as the other half are male, too. She has five sons.

96. Nine children.

97. Three more brothers than sisters. Ann's brother has one more brother than sister. Ann is one of the sisters, so Ann will have one fewer sister than her brother has and one more brother than her brother has.

98. Seven. The only possible solution is that the person talking is a woman and there are four women and three men.

99. The doctor is a woman.

100. John is Raymond's son.

101. Your mother.

102. The son's mother.

103. The second man is Charles's grandson.

104. No, because it would be his mother.

105. The man is Ann's uncle.

106. If the man left a widow, then he is dead. Therefore, he cannot get married.

109. Two widowers have one daughter each and decide to marry each other's daughters. This conversation takes place once they are married and with children. Their wives are the ones talking.

LAUGHS

273. It is possible to predict it. That doesn't mean that he is right in his predictions.

274. This puzzle is based on an old joke. What really happened was that the young man kissed his own hand and then slapped the older man in the face.

275. There is no smoke coming out of an electric train.

276. Peacocks don't lay eggs. Peahens do.

277. A hole, for example.

278. One dozen.

279. He has a glass eye.

280. A quintet.

281. When he got married, he was a billionaire. Because of his wife's spending habits, he became a millionaire.

282. He can take out his dentures and bite his good eye with them.

283. Baby elephants.

284. During his last lap.

285. You can go in through the door.

286. The hare was lying. (The first paragraph of the puzzle gives the order.)

287. Staying up at night.

288. Wet.

289. Bicycles.

INDEX

Page key: puzzle / *solution*